JACK D. FLEER ⊠

NORTH
CAROLINA
POLITICS
AN INTRODUCTION

The University of North Carolina Press
Chapel Hill

35,569

ACKNOWLEDGEMENTS

I would like to express appreciation to persons who have helped at various stages and in different ways in the period of planning, executing, and publishing this research. Professor Donald Matthews of The University of North Carolina at Chapel Hill provided an initial word of encouragement after reviewing the proposal and outline. Eddie Lincoln, Bronah Miller, and Mrs. Emily Lincoln assisted during the research and writing stages by competently fulfilling assignments with unusual enthusiasm. The offices of the Secretary of State and the State Board of Elections were always prompt and helpful in responding to my requests for election data and information. The university and departmental administrations at Wake Forest provided a teaching schedule that accommodated work on the manuscript. The Graduate Council, through its Research and Publication Fund, granted financial assistance. Others made contributions for which I am grateful.

A constant source of encouragement and assistance was my wife, Martha, who contributed in ways too numerous to mention. In conjunction with my two children, John Charles and Katherine Stuart, she provided a home environment which made research possible and enjoyable.

None of these persons is responsible for errors in the book. If any reader finds errors, I hope he will be kind enough to inform me of them. Suggestions for improvement of the scope and content of the book are also welcomed.

CONTENTS

LIST OF FIGURES

LIST OF TABLES

INTRODUCTION

The North Carolina Constitution states in Article I:

> That all political power is vested in, and derived from the people; all government of right originates from the people, is founded upon their will only, and is instituted solely for the good of the whole.

Thus, the fundamental law of the state creates a republican form of government in which government is based on popular sovereignty and is composed of representative institutions. The existence of republican and democratic government is guaranteed for every state by the United States Constitution.

In order to secure this objective of democratic republican government, many institutions and arrangements have been devised. Voting rights have been determined, political parties created and reorganized, and campaigns waged and regulated to provide the instruments and means of popular control. The focus of this book is the politics of North Carolina since 1940. A better knowledge of the structure and nature of competition for popular control and representative government is the main objective. This objective is achieved by examining major features of the state's electoral system in the last quarter century.

The knowledge of politics in North Carolina is not only useful to the professional students of politics: political scientists and politicians. Knowledge and understanding of the foundations of political power are critical to individual citizens for two reasons. On them the citizen can base a more enlightened participation in the political system. Equally important, the citizens can determine the

1

INTRODUCTION

The North Carolina Constitution states in Article I:

> That all political power is vested in, and derived from, the people; all government of right originates from the people, is founded upon their will only, and is instituted solely for the good of the whole.

Thus, the fundamental law of the state creates a republican form of government in which government is based on popular sovereignty and is composed of representative institutions. The existence of republican and democratic government is guaranteed for every state by the United States Constitution.

In order to secure this objective of democratic republican government many institutions and arrangements have been devised. Voting rights have been determined, political parties created and recognized, and campaigns waged and regulated to provide the instruments and means of popular control. The focus of this book is the politics of North Carolina since 1940. A better knowledge of the structure and nature of competition for popular control and representative government is the main objective. This objective is achieved by examining major features of the state's electoral system in the last quarter century.

The knowledge of politics in North Carolina is not only useful to the professional students of politics: political scientists and politicians. Knowledge and understanding of the foundations of political power are critical to individual citizens for two reasons. On them the citizen can base a more enlightened participation in the political system. Equally important, the citizens can determine the degree to which and the manner in which the constitutional principle of popular government is achieved.

The Political Terrain

Politics occurs in and develops from a social, economic, and political context that is not easily identified and readily apparent. Political issues arise from a variety of seemingly nonpolitical characteristics of the state such as the age of the population, the ethnic composition, the level of education, the type of economic bases, the level of personal and corporate income, and others.[1] Basic patterns of party competition are influenced by the division of governmental authority, the public offices that are provided, the methods of selecting people to fill these offices, and the boundaries of jurisdiction of these offices.

Politics revolves around elected offices that are established for certain constituencies. Political constituencies range in size and jurisdiction from the state to the local ward. The state serves as the political district for the executive officials, which includes the governor, lieutenant governor, attorney general, and seven members of the council of state (auditor; commissioners of agriculture, insurance, and labor; secretary of state; superintendent of public instruction; and treasurer). These ten officers are elected directly by the voters. There are no state legislative officials who are elected with the state as their constituencies. Members of the judicial branch, including justices of the Supreme Court and judges of the Court of Appeals and Superior Courts, are elected on a statewide

1. Readers who are interested in the social and economic environment of political activity in North Carolina should consult the *Atlas of North Carolina* (Chapel Hill, N.C.: The University of North Carolina Press, 1967), which was prepared under the direction of Richard E. Lonsdale.

basis. The state's two United States senators and its presidential electors are elected on a statewide basis.

The General Assembly, 120 members in the House of Representatives and 50 in the Senate, is elected from districts which the Assembly determines. Until 1966 the districts of the state House of Representatives were the 100 counties. According to the state Constitution written in 1868, each county was allotted one member in the lower house. An additional 20 representatives were apportioned to the counties on the basis of population. In 1964 the United States Supreme Court ruled in *Reynolds v. Sims* that representation in both houses of a state legislature must be based on population that is substantially equal. By 1966 the impact of this decision was felt in North Carolina, and the 300-year-old pattern of separate legislative representation for each county was abandoned.

The state Constitution gives the legislature the authority to determine Senate districts, but it sets forth two important provisions. The districts are to be revised after every decennial census and are to be, as nearly as possible, based on equal population. The state legislature took a casual attitude toward both of these provisions.[2] The Senate districts redrawn in 1963 had last been revised in 1941, and in 1961 the House was reapportioned for the first time since that year. Both Senate redistricting and House reapportionment were inconsistent with the Reynolds deci-

2. For a comprehensive survey of this subject see John L. Sanders, "Legislative Representation in North Carolina: A Chapter Ends," *Popular Government* (February and March, 1966). Also see Preston W. Edsall, "North Carolina: People or Pine Trees," in Malcolm Jewell (ed.), *The Politics of Reapportionment* (New York: Atherton Press, 1962), 98-110; and Preston W. Edsall, "Legislative Representation: The Aftermath of *Drum v. Seawell*," Part two of an unpublished paper prepared for the Duke University American Assembly on State Legislatures, April 13-16, 1967.

Figure I. STATE SENATE DISTRICTS, 1966

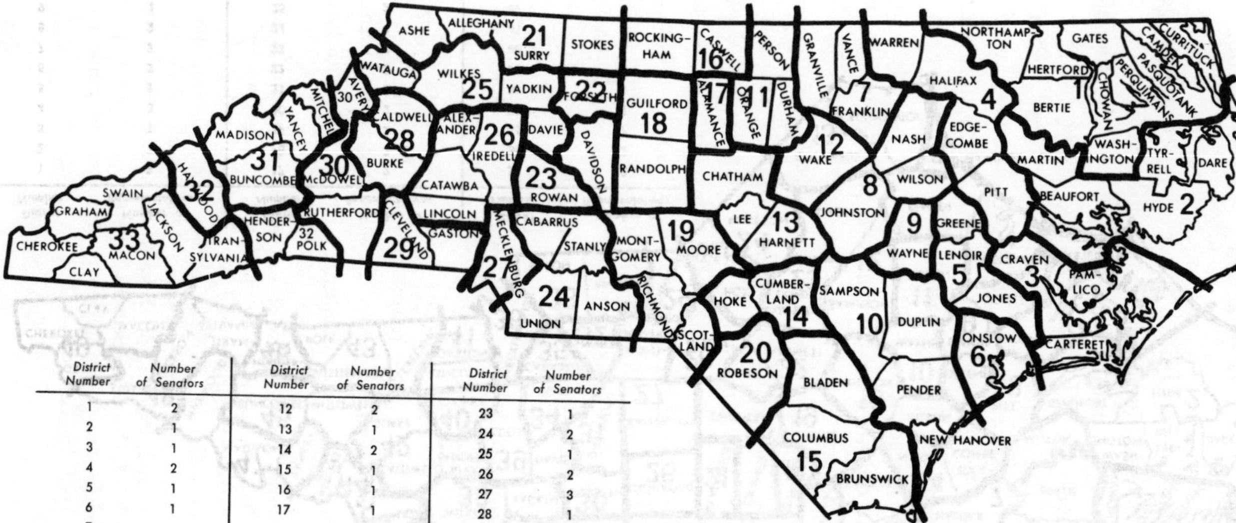

District Number	Number of Senators		District Number	Number of Senators		District Number	Number of Senators
1	2		12	2		23	1
2	1		13	1		24	2
3	1		14	2		25	1
4	2		15	1		26	2
5	1		16	1		27	3
6	1		17	3		28	1
7	1		18	3		29	2
8	2		19	2		30	1
9	1		20	1		31	2
10	2		21	1		32	1
11	2		22	2		33	1

Figure II. STATE HOUSE OF REPRESENTATIVES DISTRICTS, 1966

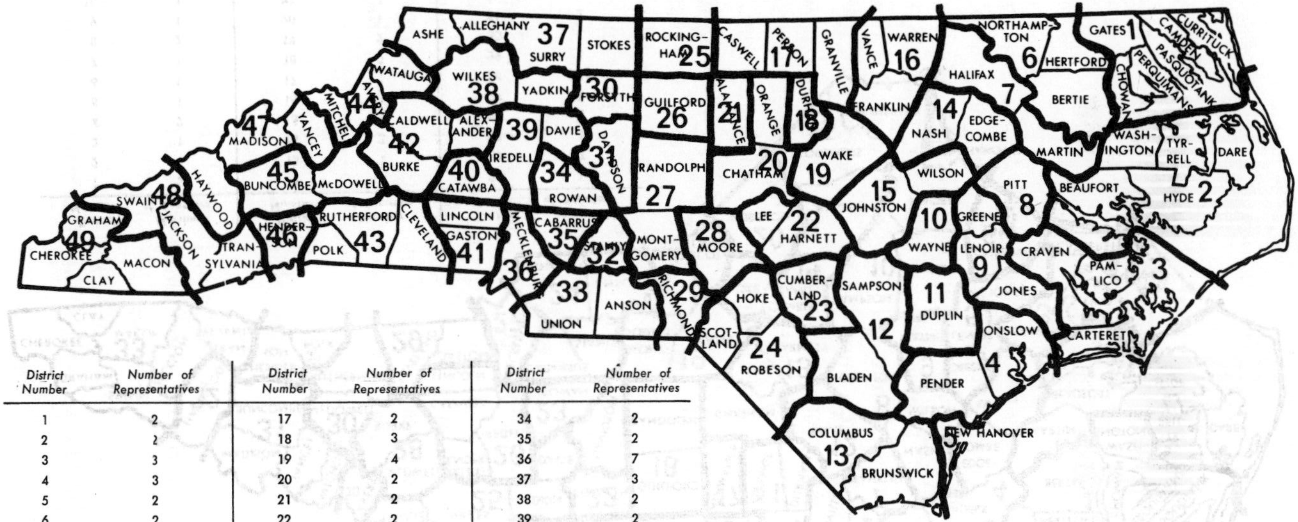

District Number	Number of Representatives	District Number	Number of Representatives	District Number	Number of Representatives
1	2	17	2	34	2
2	2	18	3	35	2
3	3	19	4	36	7
4	3	20	2	37	3
5	2	21	2	38	2
6	2	22	4	39	2
7	2	23	2	40	2
8	2	24	2	41	4
9	2	25	2	42	3
10	2	26	6	43	3
11	1	27	2	44	1
12	2	28	1	45	4
13	3	29	1	46	1
14	3	30	5	47	2
15	3	31	3	48	1
16	2	32	1	49	1
		33	2		

sion of the Supreme Court. Thus action taken by the General Assembly in special session in 1966 determined the present districts for both houses of the state legislature. Figures I and II show these districts of the House and Senate.

The 120 seats in the House of Representatives are apportioned among 49 districts composed of 1 to 6 counties each. Districts have from 1 to 7 representatives, and they range in population per member from 43,444 to 32,660 with an average of 37,968. The reapportionment and redistricting of this house contrast dramatically with what existed before. Two measures that emphasize this are population variance ratio—comparison of largest and smallest population per member—and minimum controlling percentage—the smallest percentage of people required to elect a majority of the body. Before the 1966 plan the population ratio varied 18.15 to 1; after the special session the ratio was 1.33 to 1. Prior to 1966, 27.09 per cent of the population could elect 61 members of the house; after the change, the figure was 47.54 per cent.

In the state Senate the change was not so dramatic, but it was significant. Redistricting resulted in 33 districts composed of from 1 to 10 counties and represented by from 1 to 3 senators. The average population per member is 91,123, ranging from a low of 65,722 to a high of 148,418. The population variance ratio is 1.32 to 1 as compared to 2.26 before the special session. The action changed the minimum controlling percentage from 47.06 per cent to 48.80 per cent.

The effects of these changes, particularly in the House, will take some time to show themselves. The redistribution of seats in the lower house favored the Piedmont section of the state. The eastern counties lost strength as did the west. The middle section of the state gained. Many small counties no longer have separate resident representatives in this body. In fact, the election returns in 1966 indicated that twenty-six (one-fourth) of the counties did not have representatives in the 1967 House. Nineteen counties (almost one-fifth) did not have personal representatives in either house of the state legislature. A pattern of local representation was changed dramatically by this change in basis. Of the counties without direct representation in the two houses, ten are located in the east and nine in the west. In the 1967 General Assembly all Piedmont counties had at least one representative; many had more than one.

The state legislature also has power to fix the districts of North Carolina's members of the United States House of Representatives. The power has been exercised frequently in recent years as a result of a decision of the United States Supreme Court that congressional districts should be based on substantially equal population.[3] Following the 1960 federal census, the General Assembly changed the congressional districts because the state was apportioned one less Representative than it had in 1941. North Carolina now is allotted eleven members of the lower house of Congress. The state legislature changed the congressional districts again in 1966 after the United States Supreme Court ruled in 1964 (*Wesberry v. Sanders*) that such districts should be equal in population and the United States District Court ruled that the North Carolina district did not meet this standard. The decision

3. See John L. Sanders, "Legislative Representation in North Carolina," and *Materials on Congressional Districts in North Carolina,* compiled by John L. Sanders (Chapel Hill, N.C.: Institute of Government, 1965). Also see Preston W. Edsall, "North Carolina: This Bill or Nothing," in Malcolm E. Jewell (ed.), *The Politics of Reapportionment,* pp. 191-204.

made by the General Assembly in 1966 was only temporarily satisfactory to the District Court. It ruled in *Drum
v. Seawell* that the state legislature must redistrict its
congressional seats by July 1, 1967, or the court would
do it.

When the District Court called for another attempt at
congressional redistricting by the General Assembly, it
mentioned several features of the 1966 plan which did not
meet its approval. It summarized its objections as follows:

> The tortuous lines which delineate the boundaries of
> many of the congressional districts under the proposed
> plan, the resulting lack of compactness and contiguity,
> and the failure to achieve equal representation for equal
> numbers of people as nearly as practicable compels
> [sic] us to hold that the congressional apportionment
> is constitutionally invalid.

In the closing hours of the regular session of the 1967
General Assembly, another redistricting plan was adopted,
the third since the most recent census.

In the 1966 plan, districts ranged in size from 377,293
(Third District) to 448,933 (Seventh District). The average was 414,196. Largest to smallest ratio was 1.19 to 1.
The percentage population deviation ranged from −8.91
per cent in the Third District to +8.39 in the Seventh
District. The plan received national attention because of
the caricatures which resulted from unusual shapes of the
districts.

In the plan adopted by the 1967 General Assembly the
districts have a population variation from the average
ranging from −1.86 per cent in the Fifth District to
+2.34 in the Seventh District. The population ranges
from a high of 423,750 to a low of 406,474. This plan
was approved by the special federal court on July 28,

Figure III. NORTH CAROLINA CONGRESSIONAL DISTRICTS, 1967

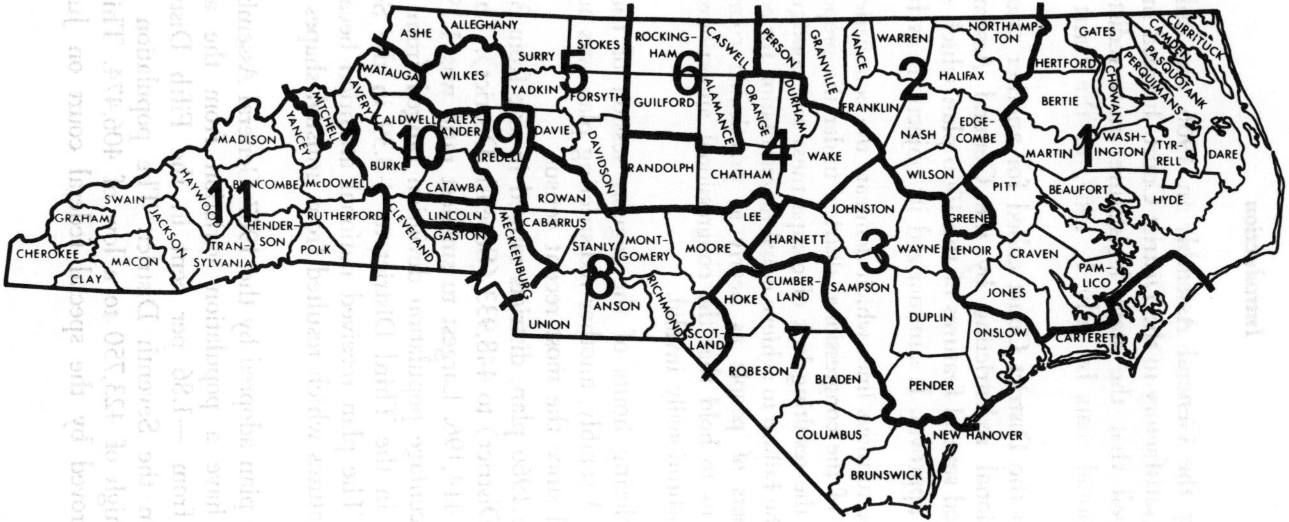

1967. The districts are indicated in Figure III. They will remain in effect until after the decennial census in 1970 when population changes might necessitate boundary changes.

CHAPTER ONE ⊠

PEOPLE IN POLITICS

People are the bases of politics. Voting is the most frequently and widely used form of political participation. This chapter examines several features of popular participation in North Carolina politics. Contemporary voting qualifications are discussed, evaluated, compared with those of other states, and viewed in historical perspective. Registration procedures are described and evaluated. Levels of registration and participation are analyzed with the object of determining their significance in the state's political system.

Qualifications to Vote

The Constitution and statutes of the state of North Carolina set forth basic requirements for voting in primary and general elections.[1] Any person who is a natural born or naturalized citizen of the United States, is twenty-one years of age, resides in the state for one year and in his voting district for thirty days, and registers, is a qualified voter providing that he can read and write a section of the North Carolina Constitution, is not an idiot or lunatic (must be of sound mind), and has not confessed to or been

1. The requirements are set forth in Article VI of the North Carolina Constitution and Chapter 163 of the General Statutes. Two very useful publications on election laws are: State Board of Elections, *Election Laws of the State of North Carolina, 1966* (Raleigh, N.C., 1966); and Henry W. Lewis, *Primary and General Election Law and Procedure—1966* (Chapel Hill, N.C.: Institute of Government, 1966).

convicted of any crime punishable by imprisonment in the state prison.

The requirements include several qualifications which are common among the states and some which are not. Age, citizenship, residence, and registration are among the requirements which North Carolina shares, except in particulars, with most other states.

Age. North Carolina shares with forty-five other states the requirement that a person be twenty-one before he is qualified to vote. The requirement must be met by the time of the general elections. Registration must be done in the regular registration period. In other words, a person who becomes twenty-one before the general election, but after the registration period ends, must register before he is twenty-one.

There has been discussion of lowering the age requirement below twenty-one. Eighteen is frequently mentioned as a desirable qualification. President Eisenhower made a proposal for changing the age requirement to eighteen in 1954. In 1963, the President's Commission on Registration and Voting Participation said: "We believe that each state should carefully consider reducing the minimum voting age to 18." However, the Congress and the states have not been eager to follow the suggestion. Similar proposals have been made in the North Carolina legislature, but there had not been serious consideration of the qualification until the 1967 General Assembly.

In that session of the legislature two constitutional amendments relating to voting age were introduced. One would have allowed the General Assembly to lower the age to a minimum of eighteen. This was rejected. The other would have lowered the voting age to eighteen and written it into the Constitution. It was approved by a vote of seventy-four to thirty-seven, two more than required to amend the constitution. But overnight the vote changed, and it was defeated, lacking nine votes of the three-fifths majority necessary. This is the closest the change has ever come to passage.

Citizenship. All states require that voters be citizens of the United States. This general requirement has existed in all states since 1926 when Arkansas changed its laws to exclude aliens from the electorate. Citizenship may be either natural born or naturalized. There is little or no controversy regarding this requirement.

Residence. To be eligible to vote in North Carolina, a person must be a resident of the state for one year and of his voting precinct for thirty days. The state residence requirement is shared by three-fourths of the states; the precinct or local residence requirement varies a great deal among the states. There is considerable discussion regarding the desirability of requiring extended periods of residence before citizens qualify to vote. In a population that is very mobile, as ours is, the residence requirement disfranchises a significant number of individuals. An estimate placed the number at 8,000,000 in 1960. Thus this requirement has a discriminatory effect.

A more realistic and less discriminatory requirement would be a state residency of six months. This would sustain the meaning and meet the need of the qualification without unduly barring a mobile population from its right to vote. The principal justifications for requirement of residence are to prevent election fraud and to increase the likelihood that voters will be informed about local candidates and issues through "exposure" over a period of time. In recent years a movement to decrease the length of residence required in voting for President and Vice President has occurred. North Carolina joined this movement in 1965. A person is qualified to vote in the state for the two national offices if he will have been a resident of the state for sixty days at the date of the general election. This is not as generous as some states have allowed, but it does seem a reasonable step in the right direction.

Residence is defined in the statutes as the domicile or intended place of living for the individual. College students, for example, who intend to return to their parents' home and who are only temporarily residing in the college community must use their home address as their legal address for voting purposes.

Literacy Test.   The North Carolina Constitution includes demonstration of literacy as qualification for voting. Article VI states that "Every person presenting himself for registration shall be able to read and write any section of the Constitution in the English language." North Carolina shared this or a similar requirement with sixteen states when such tests were challenged by The Voting Rights Act of 1965. Thus the current use of literacy test in North Carolina is subject to national legislation.

The North Carolina literacy test was upheld as constitutional by the United States Supreme Court in 1959 in *Lassiter v. Northampton County Board of Elections.* But tests of this nature are, or were, generally criticized on the grounds that they could be administered in a discriminatory fashion. That the fulfillment of the constitutional requirement varies considerably among local election boards is quite clear. A survey conducted in 1960 by the North Carolina Advisory Committee to the Civil Rights Commission indicates that practice ranges from requiring no literacy test to reading portions of the national and state constitutions. Most county election board chairmen said that they test literacy by having the individual fill out the application for registration. No standardized procedure seems to be followed.[2]

Soon after passage of the 1965 Act literacy tests were suspended in forty North Carolina counties[3] under that section of the Voting Rights Act which prohibits their use in any political unit (state or county) where less than half (50 per cent) of the voting age population were registered to vote on November 1, 1964, or voted in the Presidential election in November 1964. It is possible, according to the law, for a county to be removed from this suspension by having a court declare that it has not discriminated against Negroes in voting. There is one county (Wake) that has successfully used this procedure. The presumption that if fewer than 50 per cent of the eligible voters participated discrimination must exist has been the focus of much criticism for North Carolina officials.

United States Senator Sam Ervin, Jr., was a vigorous opponent of the law when it was adopted. Subsequently he corresponded with election officials in the counties affected by it. He concluded that "the registration and voting laws of North Carolina are administered fairly and without regard to race or color." His continued criti-

2. Sections of the state Constitution dealing with the right to vote are suggested by the state board of elections and are generally used.

3. Most of the counties are in eastern North Carolina and many are characterized by having large Negro populations. Included are the following counties: Anson, Beaufort, Bertie, Bladen, Caswell, Camden, Chowan, Cleveland, Craven, Cumberland, Edgecombe, Franklin, Gaston, Gates, Granville, Greene, Guilford, Halifax, Hertford, Harnett, Hoke, Lee, Lenoir, Martin, Nash, Northampton, Onslow, Pasquotank, Perquimans, Person, Pitt, Robeson, Rockingham, Scotland, Vance, Union, Washington, Wayne, and Wilson. Wake County was originally on the list but was removed after successfully securing exemption from the provisions of the law.

cism of the law is evident in his statement that "an un-
justified stigma has attached to almost half of our
counties." [4] Many state officials and most county election
boards in the affected localities maintain that they have not
and will not discriminate against Negroes in administering
literacy tests or other devices used to qualify potential
voters. Election officials suggest that apathy and voter
disinterest are at the base of failure to register. No federal
examiners have been sent to the state to register voters as
is permissible under the law. This, say election officials, is
because of a lack of discrimination in registration procedures.

A survey taken in 1960 shows that more than two-
thirds of the counties each had fewer than ten failures
of literacy tests. The report indicated that "almost all of
the counties reporting more than ten failures were in the
eastern portion of the state, with the heaviest nonwhite
population concentration and the lowest literacy for both
white and nonwhite." [5] In 1965 a survey taken by the
State Board of Elections substantiated the earlier findings.
It concluded that the literacy tests were not a major barrier to voting in the state. [6] The effect of the literacy test
is measured not only in the number of persons who fail.
A more important but not easily measurable feature is the
number of persons who do not attempt to register because
passage of the test is required. Some observers have reported substantial differences in rates of registration between counties that have difficult tests and counties that
do not enforce the constitutional requirement. The asso-

4. Quoted in Lloyd Preslar, "Ervin Protests Vote Test Bans,"
Winston-Salem Journal, April 21, 1966, p. 46.

5. North Carolina Advisory Committee, *Voting and Voter Registration in North Carolina, 1960* (June 4, 1961), p. 19.

6. *Winston-Salem Journal*, March 24, 1965.

ciation between a rigid test and low registration is stark.[7]

There are sixty counties that have not had the literacy test suspended, and it is therefore possible for these counties to require a demonstration of literacy. This has resulted in a double standard. However, the Voting Rights Act does regulate the procedures for administering the tests. It provides that, if a test is used, it must be given in writing to all applicants, and all records, properly identified for every applicant, must be kept for twenty-two months. The application can be used if questions about procedure arise. If a pattern of discrimination is found, a county's authority to use the test can be suspended for a period set by the court. Thus further discrimination is to be prohibited.

There are several bases for disqualification in the election laws. Excluded from the electorate are lunatics and idiots and persons who have confessed to or have been convicted of a crime punishable by imprisonment in the state prison, unless the person has his rights of citizenship restored in the legally prescribed manner. These exclusions are quite typical among the states.

Voting Requirements: Historical. The present voting qualifications in North Carolina are quite democratic compared to those the state has had in the past. While this state has not always been as restrictive as some others in regulating the right to vote, it has used many devices to limit its electorate.

The state constitution of 1776 allowed only property owners and tax payers to vote for certain offices. Free Negroes had the right to vote if they fulfilled the pre-

7. D. R. Matthews and J. W. Prothro, *Negroes and the New Southern Politics* (New York: Harcourt, Brace & World, Inc., 1966), pp. 154-55.

vious mentioned requirements. This changed in 1835 when a constitutional convention, approved by popular referendum, voted to exclude Negroes from the electorate. Property requirements were abolished by a constitutional amendment in 1857. The Constitution of 1868, which eliminated race as a barrier to voting, provided for universal manhood suffrage.

Male suffrage, predominantly among whites, continued until the turn of the century. In 1900, a constitutional amendment with the objective of restricting Negro suffrage was passed. With this action the literacy test, a grandfather clause, and a poll tax were added to the list of requirements. The grandfather clause was declared unconstitutional nationwide in 1915 (*Guinn v. United States*). The poll tax as a prerequisite for voting was abolished in 1920. North Carolina was the first southern state to take such action. The literacy test is continued in use today under provisions established by federal law.

The white primary, used to prohibit Negro participation in the nomination of Democrats for public offices, was not formally adopted as state law or party regulation in the state. In fact, however, Negroes with few exceptions, were barred from participation in the official activities of the dominant party and thus from crucial decisions in state politics. The white primary was declared unconstitutional in 1944 (*Smith v. Allwright*) and could not be used thereafter.

In response to a well organized, national campaign, Congress proposed the Nineteenth Amendment to the United States Constitution which ruled out sex as a barrier to voting. Although the North Carolina legislature turned down the demands for women's suffrage, enough other states ratified the amendment to make it effective in 1920, and women citizens of North Carolina who were otherwise qualified were permitted to vote.

Thus the present state qualifications for voting can be viewed in light of changes in the history of election laws. North Carolina has come a long way in eliminating barriers to political participation by voting, but there are still changes to be made.

Registration

As was noted earlier, registration is required for all voters in North Carolina. The procedure is designed to determine which persons are qualified, and it aids in the orderly management of voting on election day. When registering, the applicant must provide information indicating that he meets the requirements. Thus he is asked to state his name, age, place of residence, place of birth, and political party affiliation. The party designation is used to determine in which, if any, party the voter will participate. Before he can participate in a nominating primary, he must affiliate with a party. Persons who do not claim party affiliation or who declare that they are "independent" may vote in the general election, if they are otherwise qualified, but may not vote in a primary election.

Regulations for voter registration are set forth in the statutes. Actual registration is conducted by county boards of elections and precinct registrars.

Types of Registration Systems. Two types of registration systems are used in North Carolina. They are periodic registration and permanent or full-time registration. All but fifteen counties use the former.

A major difference between the two, as indicated by their names, is the period of time allowed for registration. Under a system of periodic registration the time allotted for registering is very limited. Normal procedure is for the registration books to be open from the fourth Saturday through the second Saturday prior to the primary or general election. The books are kept at the polling place only on the three Saturdays. On other days during the period, the registrar may keep the books at his residence or place of employment. In either case the books are open from 9:00 a.m. until 6:30 p.m. Therefore the books are open fifteen days before each election—thirty days every two years—for registration. However, on only six of the days are the books at a convenient, public place. (Some private places are used as polling places.)

The permanent registration systems are characterized by being more convenient and accessible to the applicant. Under these systems registration is possible "at all reasonable hours and times" during the year. However, registration less than twenty-one days before the election is not effective until after that election. Registration for all precincts within the county may take place at a permanent site, usually the county courthouse. A full-time staff generally conducts the registration. Any individual who resides in the county may be registered at any time in any place if the local board authorizes. Furthermore, once an individual is registered he does not have to re-register unless the records are lost or destroyed.

Procedure. All registration, except for absentee ballot, must be done in person. Every individual presenting himself for registration must take an oath that he is duly qualified to vote or will be by the date of the next general election. Upon completion of the oath and after satisfying the registrar of his qualifications, the individual's name and other required information are recorded in the registration book.

All persons who move from one precinct to another must make such information available to the officials in the precinct of his new residence. This procedure on transfers is necessary in order to keep the books current and accurate. It is frequently not followed, however. The consequence of such neglect is inaccurate records.

Persons who are denied registration may appeal to the county board of elections in a manner prescribed by law. The decision of the board may be appealed to the Superior Court of that county. The final recourse in such cases is the state Supreme Court.

Challenges. Any person may have his right to register or to vote challenged by another voter in the precinct. Such action may take place on either of two days—Challenge Day, the Saturday before each primary and general election, and Election Day.[8] After the voter has been informed of the reasons for his vote being challenged, a hearing is held before the precinct or county officials. If the individual is found not to qualify, his name is removed from the registration books. If the challenge is not sustained, the registrant may vote as before.

Evaluation of Registration Process. It is the responsibility of the county election boards to keep registration books accurate and current. This can be accomplished by either purging the books and/or holding a new registration. As might be expected, this responsibility is fulfilled with varying degrees of dedication and success. The law prescribes more precise means to meet the objective of accurate registration books in counties with permanent, full-time registration than in those with periodic registration. The law

8. In counties with fulltime and permanent registration, challenges may be made on one or more days per week, as established.

requires that in counties with permanent registration the names of deceased persons must be removed from the registration books upon receipt of notice of death from the register of deeds. In addition, the names of all persons who have not voted for a period of four years (six years in some counties) will be removed from the books unless the registrant can show that he is still qualified.

In discussing the adequacy of registration data, the North Carolina Advisory Committee said in its 1961 report:

> Many counties have not purged their books or held a new registration for decades. The names of those moved to other localities—to say nothing of those residing in local cemeteries—are still on their registration books. . . . Over half of the counties reported more white registrants than there are white adults residing in the counties! [9]

One county election board chairman admitted that about 8,000 names on the county's registration books should not be there. As a subsequent discussion of registration indicates, attempts have been made recently to improve the accuracy of registration records.

Difficulties with the state's registration system are not confined to the desire to have current and accurate records. Controversy surrounds two other major features of the present system. They are the limited registration period in about eighty-five of the state's one hundred counties and the prevailing type of registration system. Actually, the two matters are closely related. The briefness of the registration period—fifteen days before each election including only three Saturdays at the polling place—is felt to be unfair. When the potential registrant must seek out

9. *Voting and Voter Registration in North Carolina, 1960*, p. 4.

the books which are in the registrar's possession, he is unduly inconvenienced. In most counties certain voters may feel uneasy about visiting the registrar's home in order to register. It is likely that the system discourages registration among all potential voters.

Many observers, including two past chairmen of the State Board of Elections, would lengthen the period during which registration is permitted. What is needed is statewide adoption of the permanent, full-time system. However, some counties say they cannot afford to keep a full-time staff at a fixed location to register voters. The effects of the periodic systems of registration do deserve more serious attention and some change. Registration procedures should not be a barrier to eligibility and participation. If a citizen qualifies to vote, but does not register, he cannot vote.

Registration and Participation Levels in the State

The significance of voting qualifications and registration procedures is that they determine who will have access to the political system through means of the right to vote. Voting is the most frequent form of political participation for most citizens. Thus it is basic to the success of a democratic government.

Registration Levels. Because of the decentralized administration of registration in North Carolina, information on the subject is not easily obtained and is not uniformly determined. Both the adequacy and the accuracy of registration figures is questionable. However, figures may be used to improve our understanding of this element of state politics.

A picture of registration in North Carolina is presented in Table 1. The figures tell us a great deal about the pat-

Table 1 Number and Percentage of Voting Age Population Registered to Vote in North Carolina, 1958, 1960, and 1966

	1958		1960		1966	
	Number	Per cent voting age population	Number	Per cent voting age population	Number	Per cent voting age population
Total						
Registrants	1,832,093	71.2	2,071,780	76.4	1,934,930	75.6
White						
Registrants	1,652,658	84.0	1,861,330	90.2	1,653,796	82.4
Nonwhite						
Registrants	179,435	30.9	210,450	31.2	281,134	51.0

Sources: North Carolina Advisory Committee, *Voting and Voter Registration in North Carolina, 1960* (June 4, 1961), p. 4; and Southern Regional Council, *Voter Registration in the South* (Atlanta, 1966), p. 3.

tern of registration in the state. First, in the 1960's approximately three of four persons who meet the voting qualifications do register. This percentage is up slightly from the previous decade. Secondly, the proportion of voting age whites that was registered has fluctuated considerably. It is worthwhile to note that a smaller percentage of eligible whites was registered in 1966 than in 1958 or 1960. The real number of whites in the eight-year period varies by slightly more than 1,000. Finally, it is significant to point out that Negro registration increased dramatically in the 1960's from approximately 31 per cent in 1958-60 to 51 per cent in 1966. This span of years is characterized by the great emphasis on Negro voting rights which culminated in the 1965 Voting Rights Act.

A second set of figures highlights the fact that while the proportion of voting age Negroes that is registered has increased greatly and the proportion of voting age whites that is registered has decreased, the composition of the state's electorate has changed slightly. (See **Figure IV**.) In 1958, 90 per cent of the state's registered voters were white; 10 per cent, nonwhite. By 1966 the figures changed to 85.5 per cent white, and 14.5 per cent nonwhite.

A second important consideration in discussing registration is the party affiliation of those registered. North Carolina has a closed primary system that means only persons registered as members of a party are allowed to participate in that party's nominating primary. Party membership is generally a matter of self-determination on the part of prospective voters. Also, to register as a party member does not bind a voter to support any or all of that party's candidates in an election. Despite the laxity of eligibility regulation for party membership or registration as a party member, the data on party registration does assist in getting a better view of the state's electorate.

Figure IV.   COMPOSITION OF REGISTERED ELECTORATE BY RACE—1958, 1960, 1966

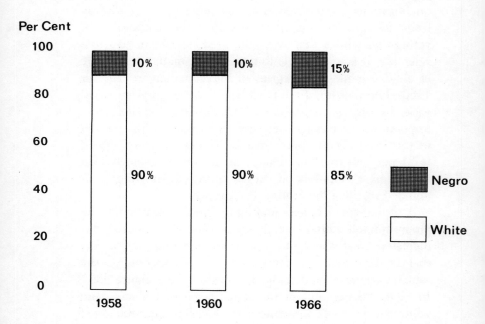

Sources: North Carolina Advisory Committee, *Voting and Voter Registration in North Carolina, 1960* (June 4, 1961), p. 4; Southern Regional Council, *Voter Registration in the South* (Atlanta, 1966), p. 3.

Registration figures by party are not easily obtained. Figures in 1966 showed that the Democrats held a four-and-a-half to one edge over the Republicans in registration. The rolls included 1,540,499 Democrats and 344,700 Republicans. By early 1967, the State Board of Elections reported that Republican registrants counted 356,869, an increase of 12,169 while the Democrats decreased by 14,424 to a total of 1,526,075. No precise figures, such as these, are available from authoritative sources on registration by party prior to recent years. In 1964, an official of the Republican party reported that Republican registration was 382,000 and Democratic registration was 1,663,000. The ratio is similar to that based on official reports, but the number of registrants is higher than that reported by authoritative sources.[10]

Registration in the Sixties. The general picture of registration of voters in North Carolina indicates that much activity has occurred in recent years. The number, racial composition, and party allegiance of registrants have changed. More insight on this subject is provided by a close look at registration by race in the one hundred counties of North Carolina. In this analysis, data on registration in 1960 and 1966 are compared. The registration for 1966 is figured as a percentage of the 1960 registration. A score of 100 per cent means that the number of registrants in the two years is exactly the same. A score of 50 per cent indicates the number of registrants is reduced to half the 1960 number. A score of 200 per cent signifies that the county has twice the number of voters registered in 1966 as in 1960. Data in Table 2 present a numerical picture of what

10. *Winston-Salem Journal,* September 9, 1964.

happened in registration by races in the first six years of this decade. First, the range of change differs significantly between the races. Registration of whites in the 97 counties on which the scores are computed ranges from a low

Table 2 Voting Registration by Race in One Hundred North Carolina Counties—1966 Registration as a Percentage of 1960 Registration

Categories of Percentages	Number of Counties in Each Category	
	White	Negro
0- 50	2	3
51- 80	29	9
81-120	55	19
121-150	11	20
151-200	0	22
201-300	0	19
301-500	0	2
501-700	0	3
Don't Know	3	3

Sources: Based on data reported in North Carolina Advisory Commission, *Voting and Voter Registration in North Carolina, 1960* (June 4, 1961), pp. 36-37; and State Board of Elections, *Registration Statistics* (July 25, 1966).

of 41 (Scotland) to a high of 141 (Swain). The picture for Negro registration is a composite of more pronounced contrast. The greatest reduction is in Jackson with a score of 9.6, while the greatest increase is in Harnett with a score of 633. In the mountain county of Jackson the numbers of registered Negroes in 1960 and 1966 respectively were 1,531 and 148. In 1960 Harnett county reported that 600 Negroes were registered. By 1966 this number had increased to 3,799. If we were to establish a range of 81 to 120 (that is a deviation of 20 per cent on either side of the 1960 figure) as a moderate change over a six-year period, we would reveal a significant characteristic of the change in registration. The registration of whites in 55 of the 97 counties falls within this range. Looking at Negro registration, we find 19 counties in the range. This supports the argument that registration of Negroes is symbolized by extreme change.

A more complete measure of the changes is provided by the number of counties in each category used in the table. The picture of white registration is principally a matter of reductions. Forty-six of the counties had a score of 90 or less. Negro registration is characterized by substantial increases. Forty-six of the counties had scores of 150 or more on Negro registration. Of this number, twenty-four counties—one-fourth of those on which figures are available—reported the number of Negro registrants had at least doubled in the six-year period.

If we look at the nature of the counties that experienced significant (double or more) change in Negro registration, we learn several additional facts. Fifteen of the twenty-four had Negro populations of 40 per cent or more. Seventeen of the twenty-four are located in eastern North Carolina. Fourteen of these counties had their literacy test suspended after the 1965 Voting Rights Act.

The changes in number of registered voters is very likely the product of many factors. Several appear most important. The period mentioned saw many laws, marches, and speeches that called for greater accessibility of registration by Negroes. Literacy tests were suspended in many counties. The general focus on equal voting rights for all races produced an environment which was more sympathetic toward eliminating discrimination. This resulted in a change in attitude toward voting rights which likely involved a purging of the registration books. This latter act resulted in the names of unqualified persons being removed from the books. The more literal interpretation of legal requirement and the concern for more accurate record keeping combined to produce changes in registration for both races.

A need for more accurate, updated records was made manifest by the study of the North Carolina Advisory Committee on voter registration in the state. Using 1960 figures on potential (voting age) voters and registered voters, the study revealed that in fifty-seven counties the number of registered whites exceeded the number of potential whites. In six counties a similar finding was noted for Negroes. Three counties had less than half of their potential white voters registered. Sixty-six counties are reported as having less than 50 per cent of their potential Negro voters registered.[11] It is clear from these figures that voter registration in North Carolina deserves a careful examination.

Voting Turnout. It is generally assumed that people register in order to vote, and the voting turnout is an important aspect of the democratic system. It is affected by both the qualifications for voting and the procedure for registration. Having discussed both factors, the subject of voting turnout can now be examined.

The pattern of voting turnout in North Carolina has remained relatively stable over the past decade and a half, since 1952 (Table 3). If turnout in presidential elections is considered, slightly more than half (51.7 per cent) of the voting age electorate has cast ballots for the top of the ticket. The relative stability in turnout which characterizes this state's electorate is duplicated at a higher level by the national electorate. Just over 60 per cent (62.2 per cent)

11. *Voting and Voter Registration in North Carolina, 1960*, pp. 6, 36-37.

of the potential national electorate voted in the period 1952-64. Participation by the electorate in the former southern confederate states has been increasing steadily and significantly in the period. In 1952, 37 per cent of the voting age population in these eleven states voted for President. By 1964 the number increased to 48 per cent. This is a dramatic change and supports a contention that the South is becoming more like the nation. The South makes

Table 3 Per cent of Civilian Population of Voting Age Casting Votes for Presidential Electors: the U. S., the South, and North Carolina—1952-64

	1952	1956	1960	1964
Per cent of voting age casting ballots—the U. S.	63	60	64	62
Per cent of voting age casting ballots—the South (states of the Confederacy)	37	36	40	48
Per cent of voting age casting ballots—North Carolina	53	48	54	52

Sources: North Carolina Advisory Committee, *Voting and Voter Registration in North Carolina, 1960*, p. 30, with supplemented information on 1964 election derived from Republican National Committee, *The 1964 Elections* (October, 1965), pp. 64-65.

an increasingly larger contribution to the national electorate, but it still has a way to go.

By viewing the national, southern, and North Carolinian voting turnouts from a different direction it is possible to note another pattern. That is, North Carolina has led the South in voter participation every year since 1920, with the exception of 1964. A larger proportion of eligible citizens vote in North Carolina than in any other southern state. However, in 1964 the leading place was occupied by Florida, not North Carolina. In Florida 53 per cent of the potential electorate voted. In North Carolina, 52 per cent voted.[12]

The pattern of voting turnout in North Carolina deserves closer examination because important differences do exist within the state. The most accurate data are available from the 1960 election because they are based on the 1960 decennial census. Counties with the highest proportion of potential voters who do participate are located principally in the western and central sections of the state, although a few are scattered in the east, particularly along the Atlantic Coast. If we divide the state into quarters and compute the average turnout and location of the high and low quarters we can get a clearer picture of the turnout pattern. The twenty-five counties with the highest proportion of voting age population casting ballots are all located in the western half of the state, most of them in the mountains. They have an average turnout of 85.6 per cent. All counties which are in the lowest quartile are located in the eastern half of the state. The average turnout in these counties in 1960 was 35.4 per cent. Figure V provides details of this pattern.[13]

Variations Relative to Type of Election.   Generally in the United States, presidential elections attract more attention and a larger number of votes than other elections. North Carolina is no exception to this national pattern. An ever-increasing number of North Carolinians cast votes for

12. Data comes from two sources: *Voting and Voter Registration in North Carolina, 1960,* p. 30; and Republican National Committee, *The 1964 Elections* (October 1965), pp. 64-65.

13. *Voting and Voter Registration in North Carolina, 1960,* pp. 28-29.

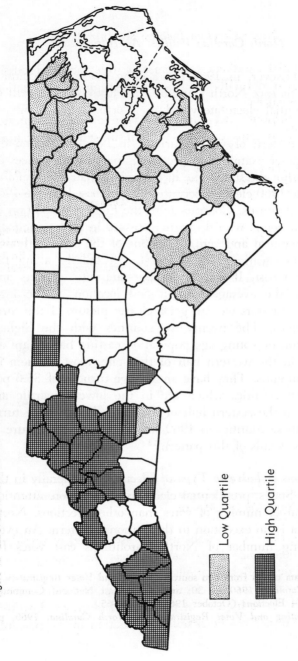

Figure V. ELECTORAL TURNOUT IN 1960 PRESIDENTIAL ELECTION—Counties in Highest and Lowest Quartiles

Low Quartile

High Quartile

Source: Based on data reported in North Carolina Advisory Committee, *Voting and Voter Registration in North Carolina* (June 4, 1961), Table 10 and Figure 3, pp. 28-29.

presidential candidates. Because of this factor, discussion of turnout normally focuses on elections of the nation's chief executive.

But turnout does vary with type of office contested. Table 4 contains data on turnout in state gubernatorial

Table 4 Turnout in Three Types of Elections in North Carolina as a Percentage of Vote in Presidential Elections, 1940-66

Year	Congressional vote as per cent of Presidential vote Presidential year elections	Off-year elections	Off-year Congressional vote as per cent of Presidential year Congressional vote	Gubernatorial vote as per cent of Presidential vote
1940	96			97
1942		36	38	
1944	95			96
1946		57	59	
1948	96			98
1950		64	67	
1952	92			97
1954		49	54	
1956	87			97
1958		52	59	
1960	95			98
1962		59	62	
1964	91			98
1966		64	70	

Sources: Based on data reported in the appropriate volumes of the *North Carolina Manual.*

and congressional elections as they are related to presidential elections since 1940. Several facts that emerge from the data deserve elaboration.

Participation in the election of the state's chief executive is almost as high as in presidential elections. Furthermore, there has not been much fluctuation in the percentage of those casting votes for President who also cast votes for governor. Approximately 97 per cent of the voters participate in election of both officials. This is not unusual since the presidential and gubernatorial elections are held at the same time. It is likely that if the state officials were elected at a time other than the President, this pattern would not exist.

A similiar finding on congressional elections held in presidential election years is supported by the data. Participation is at a lower level (mean 93 per cent) and is less stable (range 87 per cent to 96 per cent) than is the case in gubernatorial elections. This pattern reflects both lower interest and a lack of contests in some districts.

It is in off-year congressional elections when the participating electorate falls considerably short of the presidential electorate. The average turnout in elections for the state's delegation to the United States House of Representatives has ranged since 1942 from 36 per cent to 64 per cent in 1966 with an average of 54 per cent. But more significant is the decreasing difference in congressional and presidential electorates in recent years. This develops from two interrelated aspects of congressional politics. One, competition between parties for these seats is increasing. This will be elaborated in a later discussion. Second, the focus on congressional offices has increased because of more accessible and effective means of communication. Accompanying this development is the fact that the difference between the presidential-year-congressional-electorate and the off-year-congressional-electorate is also decreasing. In 1942 the turnout was 38 per cent of the 1940 congressional electorate. By 1966 the electorate had increased to 70 per cent of that in the previous presidential year.

Research on state politics across the nation reports that the higher the office the greater the proportion of the electorate which participates. This discussion of three levels of elections leads to the conclusion that this generalization is true in North Carolina. But we hasten to point out that differences between electorates for different offices are growing smaller.

Turnout in Primary and General Elections. In many southern states the Democratic gubernatorial primary attracts more attention and a larger turnout than does the general election. This pattern is not present in North Carolina.

Table 5 Comparison of Votes Cast in Democratic Gubernatorial Primary and General Elections, 1940-64

Year	Democratic primary vote	General election vote	Primary vote as a per cent of general election vote	Democratic vote in general election	Primary vote as a per cent of Democratic vote in general election
1940	470,206	804,146	58	608,744	77
1944	321,757	759,993	42	528,995	60
1948	423,125	780,525	54	570,995	74
1952	564,505	1,179,635	47	796,306	70
1956	466,654	1,135,859	41	760,480	61
1960	653,060	1,350,360	48	735,248	88
1964	769,090	1,396,508	55	790,343	97

Sources: Based on data reported in the appropriate volumes of the *North Carolina Manual.*

In the twenty-four years covered in Table 5, the mean participation in general elections has been almost double that in Democratic primaries for the office of governor.

The participation levels in the two types of elections have been quite erratic, with no definitive pattern.

This is not the case when a comparison of Democratic primary votes and Democratic general election votes is made. The data in these two columns reveal that the Democratic vote in the general election is growing increasingly closer to the number of votes cast in the Democratic primary. It is difficult to explain this development with the use of aggregate data. However, one possibility is that the Democratic party's primary electorate is growing increasingly less populated by Republicans who registered as Democrats in order to participate in a nominating election that they felt was tantamount to the final choice. Republicans may be more willing to restrict their electoral participation to the general election and their party's primary if one is held.

CHAPTER TWO

PARTY ORGANIZATION AND ACTIVITIES

Party Regulations

General Regulations of Parties. Political parties in the United States are regulated by one or a combination of the following documents: state constitutions, statutes, and party bylaws. The regulations usually extend to definition, structure, membership, elections, and finance of party. The objective is to set forth some basic, formal guidelines for the operation of parties. This chapter focuses on the definition and structure of political parties in North Carolina.

Two things must be remembered when party organization is described and examined. In almost all states the organization of parties is complex. That organization consists of a maze of committees, caucuses, and conventions that carry out party work at various levels and within different jurisdictions. Furthermore, and probably more important, it is necessary to keep in mind that formal structure as set out in the ruling document may vary from the organization in practice. In other words the real organizations in separate locales may differ because of the necessity of adapting the structure to local circumstances. In most cases the basic design will be present, but the details will vary.

Definition of a Political Party. Generally the existence of political parties is determined by a statutory definition of these organizations. North Carolina follows the practice of defining a political party and setting forth how new parties can organize to get candidates on the ballot.

A party is defined as being any group of voters that in a state general election received at least 10 per cent of the entire vote cast for governor or for presidential electors. Thus the party has to demonstrate a moderate level of support among the electorate that participated in the selection of the highest state executive officer or the slate of officers that elect the President of the United States. It is significant that these offices are used as the basis of the definition because they consistently attract the largest number of participants, are generally the most competitive, and are elected on a statewide basis.

Creation of new parties would be impossible, of course, if it depended solely on demonstrated support in previous elections. The statutes provide a procedure by which new parties are recognized. A group aspiring to be recognized as a party and thereby be entitled to place its candidates on the ballot must fulfill two requirements. It must file a petition containing the signatures of 10,000 persons who are qualified and registered to vote, who are declaring their intention to organize the party, and who declare their intention to support the new party's nominees in the upcoming election. The petition is filed with and certified by the State Board of Elections. In addition the group must hold a convention for the purpose of nominating its candidates for national, state, or congressional offices. Nominees for county offices will not be recognized until the second election after the party is certified.

Continuing electoral support must be received by the party if it is to be permitted to have candidates listed on the ballot. Any political party that does not receive 10 per cent of the vote for governor or for presidential electors will no longer be recognized as a political party in the state.

The Democratic and Republican parties have been organized in North Carolina throughout this century. Other parties have seldom emerged or continued for extended periods.

The most recent attempt to organize a new political party in North Carolina occurred in 1964. Governor George Wallace of Alabama planned to organize in several states in order to be a candidate for President. A petition with 26,000 signatures was filed and a convention was held in Raleigh. The party, named Wallace for President party, was certified. However, Wallace withdrew his candidacy and the party dissolved in midsummer when the two major party nominees were known.

A critical implication of these statutory regulations is that parties are the only proper nominators of candidates for public offices in this state. In other words, only legally recognized parties are permitted to place the names of their nominees on the ballots. Additionally, it is clear that recognition as a new party is more easily attained today than in the past. This is because the number of signatures required is decreasing in proportion to the number of eligible petitioners as the electorate grows. It would seem reasonable to conclude that the formal requirements do not bar the creation of new parties.

North Carolina law only defines political parties. The structure of party organization is not specified by law. North Carolina permits parties to determine their own structure. In this regard the state is more permissive than many others in the country.

The plan of organization for the Democratic party was adopted by its convention in January, 1964, and was revised in 1966 and 1968. The present Republican party plan of organization was adopted in 1966.[1]

1. Information on party organization is derived from the following

Organization and Activities of Political Parties

Party structure in North Carolina is divided between two types of units at each of the major levels. There are the executive structures, which are the committees, and the deliberative structures, which are the conventions. The types differ in their size, composition, method of selection, frequency of meeting, and responsibilities. This section will examine each of these factors as they relate to the several levels of party structure. The discussion is limited to the Democratic and Republican parties, the only parties that are recognized in North Carolina.

The Precinct Committee. The basic unit of organization for both political parties in North Carolina is the precinct. The precinct is not an electoral constituency for any public office. It is created for the operation of the party. Precinct boundaries are determined by the local election boards. There are approximately 2,180 in the state varying both in size and population.

Precinct committees of the two political parties are selected by party members in the precinct at a biennial meeting. This is a significant contrast to some states where precinct committees are elected in the primary. The significance in this contrast is the number and type of people who are involved. Primaries are likely to have more people participating but they are disproportionately weighted with persons who have a low level of participation in and con-

sources: State Board of Elections, *Election Laws of the State of North Carolina, 1966* (Raleigh, N.C., 1966); Henry W. Lewis, *Primary and General Election Law and Procedure—1966* (Chapel Hill, N.C.: Institute of Government, 1966); Democratic Party of North Carolina, *Plan of Organization,* 1966; and Republican Party of North Carolina, *Plan of Organization,* 1966. These plans are included in the annual editions of the *North Carolina Manual,* compiled by the Office of the Secretary of State of North Carolina.

cern about party affairs. The precinct meeting is generally sparsely attended but attracts persons who have a greater commitment to party affairs.

The Democratic party provides for precinct executive committees composed of ten "active Democrats"; the Republican precinct committees include five or more members of the party. As is the case at other organizational levels, both sexes must be represented. All members serve for terms of two years.

Each precinct committee will have a chairman, vice-chairman, and secretary. The Democratic party makes the latter officer a treasurer also. Both parties require that the two top positions be held by a man and a woman. If the chairman is a male, the vice-chairman must be a female, and vice versa.

The plan of organization of each of the parties provides that committeemen can be removed from office for several reasons including inefficiency and party disloyalty. As the plan for the Democratic party states, removal procedures can be initiated for any officer "who gives support to, aids, or helps any opposing political party or candidate of any other political party." It would be interesting to know whether this provision is enforced in both parties and how many procedures of removal have been initiated. In most cases the enforcement of this provision likely depends upon a party official's making peace with his conscience.

Meetings of precinct committees are held on call of the chairman. Their frequency depends on a number of variables including the level of competition, the existence of elections, and the degree of organization in the precinct.

The plan of organization for the Democratic party does not specify the responsibilities of the precinct committees. The Republican party plan gives its committees responsibilities in three areas: cooperate with county organization in elections and party activities, nominate members for various electoral positions like registrar and election judge, and "promote the objectives of the Party within the Precinct." This suggests that precinct committees are oriented principally towards campaigns and elections. As the "Democratic Precinct Handbook," published by the state party, admonishes:

> The two most important things that a Democratic political organization does are—
>
> 1. Get all qualified Democratic voters properly registered; and
> 2. See to it that on Election Day every Democratic voter gets to the polls to vote.

Many activities, similar for both major parties, precede and accompany these objectives of identifying their members, or at least supporters, and getting them to vote. Generally these activities include canvassing the precinct to determine the party orientations of its population, encouraging the persons who are inclined toward the party and who are qualified to vote to register, gaining the goodwill of supporters of the party, and facilitating voting by party supporters on election day.

Whether precinct party officials actually engaged in these basic activities has long been unknown. Recently several studies have provided insights into the performance of these campaign-election oriented responsibilities by local partisans.

Research on activities of precinct officials in North Carolina supplies concrete information on the activities and orientations of precinct leaders. Two separate studies were conducted in three urban areas of the state: Durham,

Greensboro, and Winston-Salem.[2] Findings on these three Piedmont areas are not necessarily representative, but do illustrate the work of precinct leaders.

North Carolina precinct officials see campaigning as the most time consuming and most important activity in which they engage. Second to this is organizational work including attending meetings and securing workers. Precinct officials infrequently participate in policy formulation and communication or candidate recruitment. When they do, these activities are considered less important than those previously mentioned.

A number of campaign activities are undertaken by precinct leaders. But some are more frequent and thought to be more helpful than others. Leaders in all three urban communities listed personal contact and communication with voters as the most frequent kind of campaigning. It is this intimate relationship which is the hallmark of precinct work, indeed, the distinctive characteristic of the party workers at this level. The personal touch remains an important ingredient in the vitality of political parties and is achieved through casual and/or more systematic canvassing.

Distributing campaign literature is another frequent activity. In performing this task, precinct workers can bring the party's message to many doorsteps and street corners. Information and policy views of the candidates and the party can be given wider circulation in a personal manner through this means.

The personal touch can also be achieved in telephone

2. This section relies heavily on the following research: Lewis Bowman and G. R. Boynton, "Activities and Role Definitions of Grassroots Party Officials," *Journal of Politics*, XXVIII (1966), 121-43 and unpublished research by Jack D. Fleer on Winston-Salem party leadership.

campaigns. This is done in the period just before the election. It allows party workers to talk to many voters shortly before they vote. In the process the party can estimate its potential strength at the polls. Also the party can offer assistance to voters that will facilitate their going to the polls on election day. Among the types of assistance that are frequently requested and offered are transportation to the polls and baby-sitting services.

An activity that commands the attention of the fewest precinct chairmen is raising and collecting funds. Money is needed for many precinct tasks, but much of the work is done by volunteers. County leaders are more directly responsible for securing political funds.

This discussion focuses on the relative use of several types of campaign activities. Such discussion must be mindful of the fact that all precinct officials do not engage in all types. In fact several students of local politics have been astounded at the low level of activity in the precinct. As one study reports:

> . . . for all their reputation as "vote-getters," local party officials do not efficiently utilize the techniques at hand to maximize the vote in their districts nearly to the extent that one is often led to believe.[3]

While precinct leaders work under directions from county party officials, they also engage the services of volunteers who work at their command. A substantial majority of the respondents in the three areas indicated that they had assistance from volunteers. This information should not surprise those who thought that precinct leaders were directors rather than organizers. In fact, as pre-

---

3. Bowman and Boynton, p. 133.

cincts get larger, the amount of direction by leaders at this level will undoubtedly increase. Precincts in urban areas are not equally populated, but they are getting large enough to require increasing numbers of party workers, both captains and foot soldiers.

County Committees: Structure.   Executive committees at the county levels differ in their organization and composition. The Democratic and Republican parties set forth these committees—their structure and functions—in the party plans and organization.

DEMOCRATS. County committees for the Democratic party include representatives of various elements of the county's party membership. Members of the county committee include: chairman and vice-chairman of the precinct committee, and one representative each from the county's Democratic Women's Club and Young Democrats. This group meets in each election year to select the county executive officers, which include a chairman, one to three vice-chairmen, a secretary, and a treasurer. The officers need not be members of the committee, but serve as ex-officio members with power to vote, except at organizational meetings. The officers serve in the place of the committee when it is not in session.

The committee fixes a common date for holding precinct meetings and a date for holding an organizational meeting of the newly elected members of the county committee. It assists in recommending party members to serve on the County Board of Elections.

The chairman and treasurer of the county committee are given specific duties. The chairman is responsible for furthering the best interests of the party through instructional classes for precinct committees and other party workers and by providing necessary materials for the party's successful operation. The treasurer's duties include raising funds to support the party's activities in the county.

REPUBLICANS. County executive committees for the Republican Party are composed and selected in a quite different manner than those of the Democratic groups. The county convention in its biennial meeting elects a committee of at least five members and three or more officers (chairman, vice-chairman, secretary). All committee members serve for two-year terms.

Financial affairs of the county are managed by a finance committee appointed by the county executive committee. It is composed of a finance chairman, three or more members, and the chairman of the county executive committee. To some degree, the responsibility for the finances of the party is separated from the executive committee. An auditing committee, appointed by the county executive committee and composed of at least three members, reviews the financial records of the county organization and makes an annual report to the executive committee.

In addition to the selection of members of these special groups, the county committee is responsible for the general conduct of party activities within its jurisdiction. Included in its duties, under the leadership of the chairman, are periodic reports to the state party on the status of the county party.

County Committees: Activities. The county executive committee and its chairman have developed as a significant focal point in the organization of state and national political parties. This is due partially to the scope of their jurisdiction. It is both narrower and broader in its responsibilities, and benefits from being at this peculiar juncture in party hierarchy.

The jurisdiction of county organizations is narrower than that of the state committee. It is not so remote as to encompass all activities within the boundaries of the state. Thus it derives significance from having closer association with individual voters than can develop from the more personal relationship possible at the county level.

But to have too narrow a jurisdiction might also limit significance. In this case the county committee has an advantage over the precinct organization. The precinct is a relatively small jurisdiction. The county organization is a combination of precincts. From the accumulated strength of these smaller units comes the significance and strength of the county organization.

County party organizations have responsibilities for the continuing operation of the party within their boundaries. Among the duties performed primarily by county leaders are dispensing patronage, recruiting candidates, raising money, and directing and managing the organization.

Since the precinct is not a constituency and there are few ward or city committees, the county is the lowest constituency in governmental structure that has a party organization. Many officials are elected from within its boundaries, and many state and federal activities are carried on with the county as a basic administrative unit. While there is a decreasing amount of patronage available, much of what is available is dispensed at the county level through county committees. In a one-party state the availability of patronage is likely to be unbalanced. A recent survey found that 80 per cent of the Democratic county chairmen dispensed patronage positions in North Carolina, and 90 per cent of the Republican chairmen had no patronage at their disposal. Most (68 per cent) political appointments available to counties were from state and federal sources. Seven of eight appointments by Republican chairmen derived from federal sources.[4] Patronage is not abundant at the county level, but it does exist, especially for the majority party.

Among elected officials in the counties are commissioners, sheriff, register of deeds, clerk of superior court, treasurer, and coroner. In addition, until 1966 the county was the constituency for all members of the state's House of Representatives. Today the county is a basic unit for the districts of members of both houses of the General Assembly, members of the United States Congress, and several state judicial positions. In addition many local officials are elected within the counties. In other words, many offices must be filled, and this involves recruiting candidates. County committees and their chairmen frequently shoulder the responsibility of seeking persons from their party to run for these elective positions.

Most efforts will be focused on county and state legislative candidates with less attention being given to persons who would serve in municipal, congressional, and statewide offices. A study of county chairmen in North Carolina reports that Democratic county chairmen are less likely to be involved in the recruiting process, while chairmen from the minority party see this as a frequent responsibility. As may be expected Republican chairmen experience greater difficulty in recruiting potential party standard bearers. The data reveal that from one-third to one-half of the Republican leaders at the county level confront problems

4. William J. Crotty, "The Role of the County Chairman in the Contemporary Party System in North Carolina," unpublished Ph.D. dissertation, The University of North Carolina at Chapel Hill, 1964, pp. 105-6.

in seeking candidates. The greatest problems are for offices at the lowest levels and for judicial posts. In the minority party there is usually a smaller number of potential candidates, and, of course, there is usually less assurance that the candidates will be victorious. Thus Republican candidates may have to be drafted and frequently are.[5]

County committees occupy pivotal positions in assuring financial support for the party. They provide the superstructure for raising and distributing funds at the local level and for meeting part of the financial requirements of operating a state party organization. Most contributions for county political activities must come from within the county, although occasionally the state and national parties will supplement the funds which can be gathered by the county committee. Crotty concluded in his study that the North Carolina Democratic party manifests "a more thoroughly interdependent" structure in securing financial support for its operation. On the other hand the average Republican county committee found itself in a state of "financial isolation," neither giving a great deal to the state party nor receiving much aid from it.[6]

Finally, county committees are involved in directing and managing the party organizations within their jurisdictions. This responsibility includes a plethora of activities which may be divided into two categories: general organizational matters and activities that are more directly related to the campaign and election.

The first category includes manning the organization, maintaining party morale and interest, and identifying and recruiting supporters. The county committee serves as a link between the party and the voter. To assist its opera-

5. This discussion relies heavily on Crotty, pp. 107-17.
6. *Ibid.*, p. 157.

tions, it must organize the precincts and secure personnel to function at both levels. This includes both precinct committee members and party workers.

In this regard, the health of party organization is reasonably good. A 1962 survey found that the Democratic party was organized in all one hundred counties, while Republican county organizations existed in ninety-five counties. In more than three-fourths of the counties the Democrats had all precincts organized. Republican organizations were reported in all precincts of thirty-five counties. Other aspects of organization were also examined. These included record-keeping and frequency of meetings. The survey concluded that one-fourth of the counties have a high level of organization, one-third have a moderate level of organization, and two-fifths have a low level of organization. In summation the study states:

> . . . the Democratic party is *more consistently* organized statewide than is the Republican party. The Republicans show a greater tendency to swing from very high levels of organization to very low levels.[7]

The minority party is more likely to concentrate its organizational efforts on fewer counties creating very vital structures which have some hope of success. Undoubtedly, the level of Republican organization has increased since this survey.

A political party is a social organization. Its members associate more or less frequently. They must have a program which attracts their attention and keeps up their spirit. The leadership must communicate with the workers and followers; between campaigns and during campaign

7. *Ibid.,* pp. 96-97.

battles, the needs of party members must be met. Regular meetings, workshops, speeches, publicity, and socials—all contribute to this regular function of the county committee. Committees, naturally, vary in the devices used and in devotion to this function. But a healthy political unit does require a supporting social structure.

The public must also receive the continued considera-tion of the party organization. Included in this aspect of the program are canvassing, registration drives, and gen-eral public appeals. All eligible and potential voters should be contacted, and if party supporters are found they should be registered. This operation will likely be carried out by precinct leaders and workers under the direction of the county committee, particularly the chairman. Then the party must make a general appeal for support. A sympathe-tic environment for the party must be created among the many people whose only political activity is occasional casting of ballots. This basic supportive attitude can then be heightened at the time of the campaign and election when specific candidates and issues are competing for voter support.

The second category of activities includes the many campaign and election day tasks which surround a par-ticular contest for public office. The tasks consume greater time and energy of many more people than must ordinarily be devoted to between-campaign activities. In the period of four to six months before election day, the rather calm and dormant party headquarters is converted into a bustle of activity that culminates on voting day. At this time the organization should be running at full capacity and accel-erated velocity. This is the exciting period of party work.

The county committees are instrumental primarily in giving direction to the party precinct organization and in assisting the party candidates, individually or collectively, in waging their campaigns.[8] The extent of their direction and assistance varies. A sample of opinions expressed by county chairmen in North Carolina concluded that the likelihood of a county committee being engaged in campaign activities is related to the level of office contested. Involvement decreases as one moves down the hierarchy of governmental offices. The order, from highest to lowest, is President, governor, United States Congress, state legislature, county commissioners, other county offices, local officials, and judicial officials.[9] It is of interest that county committees do not give priority to county offices.

A basic difference between the two major parties is evident in campaigning, as it was in level of organization. The Republican party is more likely to have intense campaigning in a few select locations and for fewer offices than the Democrats. The majority party competes for virtually all offices throughout the state. The Republicans, in attempting to build their party, must concentrate their attention on offices and locations where success is possible.

District Organizations.   In the electoral organization of state governments there are many constituencies which include more than one county but do not extend to the state's boundaries. These political subdivisions are the districts from which members of the state legislature, United States House of Representatives, and state judicial branch are selected. In North Carolina there are five types of political districts in this general category.[10] They are

8. See the discussion of specific activities, *infra,* Chapter Three, pp. 61-79.

9. Crotty, p. 134.

10. The fifth type became necessary when districts including more than one county were used as the basis of representation in the North Carolina House of Representatives in 1966.

legislative districts for both houses of the General Assembly, solicitorial districts, judicial districts, and congressional districts. The Republicans and Democrats provide for party organization of these political subdivisions in their respective plans of organization.

· The Republican party's district committees for state legislative and judicial offices are composed of persons appointed by the several county chairmen and approved by the county conventions in the district. Each committee selects its own officers before each state convention. Committees are responsible for recruiting candidates for the various offices and assisting candidates in their campaigns.

The Republican congressional district committees are composed of officers selected at a biennial district convention, all county chairmen in the district, county vice-chairmen for counties that gave majorities to Republican presidential or gubernatorial candidates in the preceding election, and others if so provided. A district finance committee is organized to raise funds to support the congressional campaigns.

All district committees of the Democratic party are organized and selected by delegates from counties in each congressional district to the state convention. All counties have two committee members, except counties in districts that have fewer than five counties. They get three members on the district committees. The officers of these committees are appointed by the chairman of the state executive committee immediately after the state convention. In districts that are composed of only one county, the county committee serves concurrently as the district committee.

In both parties the chief duties of the district committees are to recruit candidates, raise funds, and assist the candidates in the organization and conduct of their campaigns.

State Committees: Structure. At the top of the party structural hierarchy are the state committees. The two state committees vary in size, composition, representativeness, method of selection, and specific responsibilities.

The Democratic state executive committee is composed of ten men and ten women from each congressional district. Members are selected by delegates from counties comprising the district who meet prior to each state convention. An important qualification to this general rule exists: each county in the district must be represented on the committee. The formal rule calls for the committee to select its own officers, chairman and vice-chairman. In reality, these choices are frequently made by the governor or gubernatorial nominee in the next general election. The party's two national committee members and two national committee members of the Young Democrats serve ex-officio on the committee but are allowed to vote.

The Republican executive committee is larger and more broadly representative. Its composition is potentially quite cumbersome for effective operation. Included are:

1. Representatives from congressional districts, including the chairman, vice-chairman, and national convention district delegates and district presidential elector chosen at the district convention.

2. State officers (chairman, vice-chairman, secretary, assistant secretary, treasurer, finance chairman, general counsel) and two representatives to the national committee.

3. Immediate past officers (chairman, vice-chairman of committee, and chairman and secretary of preceding state convention).

4. Representatives of Young Republican Federation and Republican Women's Federation.

5. Republican congressmen, legislators, and members of the State Board of Elections.

6. Chairmen from counties that gave a majority vote to their Republican presidential or gubernatorial candidate.

7. Vice-chairman from counties which gave a majority vote to both Republican presidential and gubernatorial candidates.

The committee is quite obviously structured to reward those segments of the state that are most loyal to the party. The vast majority of the committee will be composed of members representing the predominantly Republican areas of the state.

The potential size of this committee makes it necessary for the Republican party to provide a smaller group called the state central committee. It includes the congressional district chairmen, state officers and national committee members, chairman of Young Republican Federation and Republican Women's Federation, and Republican leaders in state Senate and House.

The chairman and vice-chairman of the executive committee are selected at the state convention and serve in the same capacities on the central committee. Other state officers are selected by the executive committee.

As at other levels in the Republican party, a finance committee is organized at the state level. It consists of representatives from each congressional district and the chairman of the state party. A finance chairman is selected by the state executive committee to serve at its pleasure.

Party Activities at the State Level.   State committees have general authority over the operations of the party throughout the state. Their primary objective, however, is election of party nominees to statewide positions. In meeting this objective they do concern themselves with party organization at lower levels. Generally this concern does not extend to having specific direction and control of local party affairs. Indeed, it is not unusual for a county committee to find itself at odds with the state committee. If it does, it may voice its disapproval and withhold its support without fear of reprisal.

Both parties have state organizations which comply generally with the plans discussed earlier. The Democratic party organization is housed in a permanent headquarters in the state capital. Its address is:

State Democratic Executive Committee
Hotel Sir Walter
Raleigh, North Carolina 27602

The Republican party headquarters are located at the following address:

North Carolina Republican Party
Carolina Hotel
Raleigh, North Carolina 27602

The activities of the state party executive committees are varied and change from year to year as the political climate changes. But certain duties and responsibilities are enduring and require much attention from the chairmen and their assistants. The first is maintenance of a state party headquarters.

The chairman is directly responsible for the operations of the state party. He is assisted by several subordinates who carry on the day-to-day routine of the party. The Democratic party headquarters' staff is headed by a full-time executive director. Other personnel, both full-and part-time, include a director of youth activities and several typists. In the period around election the size of the staff may increase as new demands are placed on the state headquarters.

The Republican party has recently changed the site and nature of its state headquarters. In mid-1967 a headquarters in Raleigh was created and a staff assembled. An executive secretary directs research and clerical staffs. Like the Democratic party, the staff is likely to increase as campaigns approach.

Republican plan of organization states that the executive committee should meet at least annually, and the Democratic state executive committee is required to meet in early January of every election year, that is, biennially. These and other meetings of the committee are held at the call of the chairman.

Among major responsibilities carried on by the committees, with the chairman leading and the staff assisting, are campaign activities, fund raising, and planning the convention.

CAMPAIGNING.   Once the nominees are determined, the forces of the state party are devoted to the campaign of candidates for state offices and others, such as national ticket and congressional ticket. The newly chosen gubernatorial nominee can generally assure the cooperation of the state party by exercising his prerogative to select the party chairman.

The plan of organization for the Democratic party provides for a state campaign committee that is composed of two persons (a man and a woman) from each congressional district. The committee works with the state chairman to coordinate the activities of the many units of the party.

One event which has become traditional in the Democratic party is the congressional campaign rally. A rally is held in each district in the two-month period before the election every two years. At each rally the district's Democratic congressional candidate appears with the incumbents and/or candidates for state offices (governor and council of state) and other local candidates. Much speech-making and politicking occurs to arouse enthusiasm for the party's candidates. The facilities and operations of the state party are focused on the gubernatorial campaign and other state offices. The campaign of the gubernatorial candidate may be separated from the state party, but the latter does supplement the candidate's organization. It is not unusual for the state party chairman to be the campaign manager for the gubernatorial nominee.

Republican party campaigning at the state level is coordinated by the executive committee with specific duties assigned to the officers of the committee. Until recently the chairman, vice-chairman, national committee members, secretary-treasurer, and general council were each charged with responsibilities for managing the campaign for specific state executive and judicial offices until permanent campaign managers are selected. Now the chairman has overall responsibility and specific concern for the campaigns for governor and lieutenant governor.

FUND RAISING. Political parties use many means of raising funds for their operations. Among the most successful devices, in terms of low overhead and proportionately high intake with a definite time for collection, is the political dinner. Each state party stages events which may be billed "banquets for billfolds." The dinner is an important social event in the life of a party and provides a congenial atmosphere for exchanging political ideas. But the primary reason for its existence is as a fund-raising device.

The Democratic state party sponsors two fund-raising dinners each year. The Jefferson-Jackson Day dinner is held in the spring in the state capitol, and recognizes two important national figures in the history of the party. Tickets to the dinner cost $50 per plate. In addition to the meal the guests can hear a speaker of national or international reputation extol the virtues of the party.

The other affair is the Vance-Aycock dinner which is held in late summer or fall in Asheville. The location is fixed to provide a significant party event that is more accessible to people in western North Carolina. The fare and focus of the dinner differ from that previously described. Donations of $25 are expected. The dinner commemorates two North Carolina Democrats who are held in esteem by the party. Zebulon B. Vance was twice governor of North Carolina: 1862-65 and 1877-79, in which year he was elected to the United States Senate; and Governor Charles B. Aycock (1901-5) holds a special place in the history of the party because of his emphasis on education. The focus on the state is observed in selecting a North Carolinian to address his fellow Democrats.

Republican dinners are also held from time to time to raise funds. The dinner to recognize party leaders is the Lincoln Day dinner, which is held throughout the nation in the late winter or early spring. No specific state dinner is held on a regular basis. Occasionally, however, the party will convene to recognize one of its former leaders or an incumbent office holder. The event permits the party coffers to swell and party members to socialize.

An activity that may or may not be related to fund-raising dinners is the quota system. Both parties assign quotas to each county unit of the party. Quotas are based on the number of registered and voting party members in the county. Crotty reports that in the early sixties county quotas ranged from "negligible sums ($10 or $20) to quite sizeable ones ($5,000 to $8,000)." The average county assessments in early 1960's were Democrat $942.71, Republican $533.38.[11]

The party units vary in meeting the quotas. Only six Democratic county committees reported not paying their exact quota: four exceeded the quota, and two fell short of theirs. A phenomenal 88 per cent of the counties did their share, no more and no less. The Republican record is not so satisfactory. That party's county units contributed in the following manner: 25 per cent gave the exact quota; 54 per cent did not meet the quota with some of them falling very short; and 21 per cent exceeded their quotas, in some cases five- to ten-fold.

CONVENTION. The state committees have the responsibility of planning the biennial state conventions. The committees determine the time and location of the convention and make other arrangements for the conduct of the convention.

The purposes and business of the conventions of the two state parties are similar, although not identical. They can be divided into three categories: selecting officers and nominees, drafting the party platform, and arousing enthusiasm for the party.

The Republican convention selects the chairman and vice-chairman of the party and the two National Committee members. Conventions in both parties select delegates to the national convention every four years. In addition, each party convention selects two nominees for at-large presidential electors who will be chosen in the general election in presidential years.

11. This and subsequent data is based on Crotty, pp. 166-69.

Generally in the past, the Republican state convention was the place for choosing the party's nominees for state offices. In 1964 a primary was used to determine the party's gubernatorial nominee.

Each state convention adopts a platform that expresses the party's policy positions. Previous to the convention's consideration a platform committee studies policy proposals and recommends planks to the convention. Frequently adoption of the platform will provide much of the fireworks of the convention as different elements of the party compete to have their views embodied in the document. Occasionally this results in the platform being less meaningful in the campaign.

Mixed with the serious business of personnel selection and policy expression is the necessity of arousing enthusiasm for both and for other party activities. Thus, the convention frequently takes on the air of a campaign rally with characteristic excitement and expectation. The convention provides an opportunity for major and minor party figures to get together, exchange ideas, make plans, develop strategies, and generally rail against the opposition and reaffirm the virtues of the party. Much of the railing and reaffirming is done from the podium where numerous speakers, headed by a keynoter, attempt to hold the attention of the delegates, to stir their emotions, and to challenge them to harder work for the party.

Other activities will be undertaken by the state party as the need demands. Both state organizations conduct workshops from time to time to inform and train party workers on the latest techniques of campaigning. There is need for communicating with party workers. The Democratic party recently began publishing the *Tar Heel Democrat,* a quarterly, whereas the Republican publication is the *GOP Newsletter.*

Sometimes the party chairman may be involved in recruiting candidates for offices at various levels. This has been a frequent responsibility of the Republican party leader in recent years. Activities in the state legislature may also attract the attention of the state organization. In both parties the state chairmen will be in frequent contact with the party's legislative leaders to discuss party program and strategy. Twice recently the Democratic state chairman served as the governor's legislative liaison.

Always, of course, the state party is represented by the chairman who serves as its spokesman. The chairman must fill many speaking engagements with local party organizations and civic groups. After every election the chairmen are called upon to assess the results. Every major legislative battle in which parties differ includes statements of their contrasting positions by the state chairmen. The state chairman frequently represents his party in national party councils. This responsibility as the official voice of the party enables the chairman to have a considerable impact on the public image of the party. Many people view the state party through the chairman.

Deliberative Structure

Precinct Meetings. Every two years at a time designated by the state parties, precincts hold meetings for the purpose of electing the precinct committees and selecting delegates to the county convention. The number of delegates selected is based on formulas set forth in the plans of organization. In both parties one vote is allotted for every fifty votes, or major fraction thereof, cast in the precinct for the party's nominee for governor in the previous general election. In the Democratic party every precinct is given two voting delegates regardless of the number of votes cast for its nominee in the precinct. To explain the formula, an example is given. In a given precinct 400 votes are cast, 250 for the Democratic gubernatorial candidate and 150 for the Republican. The Democrats in the precinct would be allowed five votes in the Democratic county convention. The Republican precinct meeting would select delegates to cast three votes in the Republican county convention. These formulas are based on incentive to reward precincts for getting out the party vote.

In addition to selecting delegates, the Democratic precinct meeting can, under the plan of organization, discuss and vote on matters that are to come before the county convention. These votes instruct delegates when they represent the precinct in the convention.

Even though all precincts are allotted votes in the county convention, some may go unrepresented. If the party organization in a precinct is not active, it will face difficulties in finding delegates to attend.

County Conventions.   The county convention is the next level in the hierarchy of the deliberative structure. In the Republican party the convention selects the county officers and executive committee. In each party the convention must select delegates to the state convention. Formulas of the two parties differ. In the Democratic party each county is allotted one vote (delegate) for every 300 Democratic votes, or major fraction thereof, cast for the party's gubernatorial candidate in the last election. The Republican party uses a more complicated formula:

a) Each county gets a minimum of one vote;
b) One additional vote is granted for every two hundred votes or major fraction thereof for the Republican gubernatorial candidate in the last election;
c) A bonus vote is awarded for each Republican elected

to the state legislature or to the state or national ticket from the county.

Thus, the Republican formula uses votes cast for and majorities won by the party's candidates to determine county votes. The county convention must also confirm appointments by the county chairman of its representatives on solicitorial, judicial, and senatorial committees.

Congressional District Conventions. These conventions meet periodically to select officers and representatives of the district. In the Democratic party each district selects ten men and ten women to serve on the state executive committees, with at least one person from each county. In the Republican party each district has a minimum of one member on the state committee. One additional member is allotted for every 6,000 votes or major fraction thereof cast within the district for gubernatorial candidates of the party. Delegates to the party's national convention are also determined on the basis of the number allotted by the national party. Finally each district nominates one person to serve on the party's slate of presidential electors. In the Democratic district meetings representatives are chosen to serve on the executive committees for congressional, judicial, state senatorial, and solicitorial districts. Also each district selects persons to serve on standing committees of the state convention.

The various conventions are not held solely for the purpose of selecting personnel and delegates. Each convention may consider matters of policy, adopt a platform, attend to party business, have speakers, pass resolutions, and many other items. If nothing else occurs, the conventions do provide means for bringing members of the party together.

CHAPTER THREE ⊠

NOMINATIONS, CAMPAIGNS, AND ELECTIONS

Political parties spend much time seeking public offices. Indeed, political parties dominate the electoral process in its three major elements: nominations, campaigns, and elections. In North Carolina as in other states, political parties are the principal agencies charged with the important responsibility of recruiting candidates to occupy the many public positions at all levels of government. Individuals can compete for the nominations, but the competition centers around major party nominations. Thus, parties are a vital element of the political system. This chapter examines activities surrounding this vital role and preoccupation of parties.

Nominations

Around the country more attention is generally focused on elections than on nominations. However, the decisions made at the nominating stage are just as important as those made in elections. In nominations, the many people who aspire to an office are usually decreased to two—one from each major party. Thus, in choosing the nominees, the parties structure the election decision in a very significant manner.[1]

1. Information on the regulation of nominations is derived from the following sources: State Board of Elections, *Election Laws in North Carolina, 1966* (Raleigh, N.C., 1966); and Henry W. Lewis, *Primary and General Election Law and Procedure—1966* (Chapel Hill, N.C.: Institute of Government, 1966).

Candidacy.   In order to be a candidate for a public office, a person must be nominated by a political party or fulfill requirements to be an independent candidate. There are qualifications which determine an individual's eligibility for candidacy. Four principal categories of people are disqualified from holding public office in the state of North Carolina: (1) "persons who shall deny the being of Almighty God," (2) persons not qualified to vote, (3) persons convicted for committing or confessing to a crime punishable by imprisonment in the state unless such person is properly restored to citizenship, and (4) persons who are involved in fraudulent activity in respect to voting and persons who are convicted of violating the Corrupt Practices Act or of other offenses against the elective franchise. Furthermore, no person can concurrently hold an office in the United States' government, the government of any other state, or another governmental office in this state. Thus, double office holding is prohibited. In addition, each office has specific qualifications which apply. For example, a candidate for governor or lieutenant governor must be at least thirty years of age, a United States citizen for five years, and a resident of the state for two years by the time of the election.

Only persons who are registered as affiliated with a particular party or who pledge to register with a particular party may file as candidates in the party's primary. Any person who files as a candidate must pledge loyalty to the party and willingness to support the candidates nominated by the party in its primary in the next general election. No penalty is provided, however, for persons who break the pledge.

The place and time for filing as a candidate differs according to the office. Candidates for state offices, including governor, justice of Supreme Court, judge of the Court of Appeals, judge of superior court, district court judge, United States senator, member of Congress, or solicitor, file with the state board of elections not later than noon on the Friday before the tenth Saturday before the primary. Candidates for other offices—i.e., state senator, member of House of Representatives, county or township offices—must file with the county board of elections of the county in which they reside not later than noon on or before the Friday preceding the sixth Saturday before the primary.

When an individual files for office, he must pay a fee. In most cases the fee is equal to 1 per cent of the gross annual salary of the position. Thus, the filing fee for a candidate for governor is $350; for a member of state House of Representatives, $18. The filing fee serves two purposes by helping to defray the cost of the election and by limiting filing to only those candidates who are serious about running.

No write-in candidates are permitted in a party primary. However, write-in candidates may be elected in the general elections. Independent candidates in a general election must meet certain requirements. These include filing a petition signed by 25 per cent of those entitled to vote for that office according to the vote cast in the last gubernatorial election and submitting an affidavit that he is a nonpartisan candidate who is not affiliated with any political party.

Methods. Candidates for party nomination in North Carolina are selected by one of two methods. The direct party primary is used mostly by the Democratic party, and the convention is used mostly by the Republicans. An increasing but still small number of Republican primaries are held. Also, a small number of Democratic nominations for state legislature are made by conventions.

Primaries in North Carolina are closed. That is, only persons who register an affiliation with a particular party may participate in that party's nominating primary. Even this restriction on participation in the nomination of party candidates does not limit the influences on this important step in the electoral process. The convention method of nominating puts nominations in the hands of a smaller and more actively partisan group.

In order to insure that the party's nominee has wide support as he enters the general election, North Carolina laws permit a second or runoff primary. This device is common to southern states, although the particulars are not. In North Carolina if no person receives a majority of the votes cast in the first primary, the person who receives the second largest number of votes can request a runoff between the first and second place candidates. If the request is made, the runoff is held. If not, the person who receives the highest number of votes, even though it is not a majority, is declared the winner.

Although the primary election is held for the purpose of selecting nominees for political parties, it is conducted and financed by state and local governments. Primaries are regulated in accordance with laws set forth for the conduct of general elections with necessary changes made due to difference in type of elections. While the state regulates primaries in North Carolina, it must be remembered that until the present almost all state and local officials have been members of the Democratic party. But in several other southern states the administration of primaries is strictly a party affair with no semblance of public responsibility.

Until 1968 primaries were held on the last Saturday in May before the general elections in November. The 1967 General Assembly moved the date to the first Saturday in May. Runoff primaries, if necessary, are held on the fourth Saturday after the first primary. When conventions are used for nominating, the timing and conduct is strictly a party affair.

The value of the convention as a nominating device is that this important party business is conducted by party activists in a semiprivate environment. Appeals of prospective nominees must be made in caucuses before county and district delegations rather than in campaign travels and speeches. The popular appeal necessary in the primary may result in bitter competition between candidates. Such competition, because of its public exposure, may be more difficult to smooth over than the contest conducted in the relative privacy of caucuses and convention deliberations. Because of restricted participation in conventions, many critics have charged that they are undemocratic, boss-ridden devices. This is not inevitable, but research on participation in primaries indicates that they certainly do not meet the democratic objective of widespread, representative participation set out by those individuals who proposed their adoption earlier in this century.

North Carolina does not hold a presidential preference primary. Primaries are held for state executive officials every four years, e.g., 1964, 1968, 1972. Primaries for the state legislators and members of Congress are held every two years, e.g., 1964, 1966, 1968, 1970. Primaries for local elections may not be held at the same time as those for higher levels. The frequency of local primaries will be determined by the terms which local officials serve in office. Each voter should become acquainted with his local election calendar in order to exercise his right to vote.

Campaigns and Campaigning

Having decided to seek the nomination or having been chosen as the party's nominee for office, a candidate will probably spend much time, effort, and occasionally money campaigning for votes in the election. While the general purpose of campaigning is common to all candidates, the duration, organization, and specific activities of the campaign will vary considerably. A number of factors such as nature of the office, size and character of the constituency, available resources, personality of the candidate, issues, and other things will influence the type of campaign waged.

Campaign Calendar. The duration and schedule of a campaign will be determined by a number of factors. The position being sought, the nature of competition for the position, the number of contestants, and other factors have their effects. The formal opening of the campaign comes on the filing date when all potential contestants must declare their intentions. The final date for filing as a candidate for office at the state level is the tenth Saturday before the election. For offices which file at the county level the date is the sixth Saturday before the primary.

There is no typical calendar of campaign activities. However, some patterns do exist, and illustrations will assist in understanding this element of campaigning. The campaign for the 1964 Democratic gubernatorial nomination illustrates a type of calendar.

Speculation regarding potential candidates in an election usually begins soon after the previous election. Throughout the period between elections, politicians survey the political horizon looking for prospects. Factions and groups will put forth candidates, discussing their qualifications and attributes, with the objective of testing their political appeal and strength. These tests are referred to as "trial balloons." An important consideration is whether the balloon stays aloft or falls and the duration of either.

Throughout the early 1960's balloons for various candidates were tested. By 1963 a front-running prospect in the Sanford faction was the Democratic Party Chairman, Bert Bennett. Bennett had served as Sanford's campaign manager and as chairman since 1960. Considered judgment indicated that he was a very capable politician and through his work in the Sanford campaign and administration had developed very important contacts with state and local party leaders. But by mid-1963 concern within the Sanford forces had developed over whether someone so closely associated with the incumbent governor would be a successful candidate. Also, the close ties between Sanford and the Kennedy administration, especially its civil rights program, raised questions.

By August this speculation resulted in an effort to find someone with the appropriate orientation but not the close association. Federal Judge Richardson Preyer's name was mentioned. Preyer reportedly would not consider running unless he were assured of the support of the people of Guilford County, where his home was located, and of the statewide following of Sanford and Bennett. Others mentioned at about this time were Dr. Henry Jordan, brother of the incumbent United States senator, and Thomas Pearsall, former speaker of the state House who was widely known for his "safety valve" plan for desegregation of the state's public schools. By late August, Jordan and Pearsall were out of consideration, and Preyer announced that he would be interested in running.

Meanwhile, other factions were making decisions. In the western part of the state, Dan K. Moore, from a prominent

North Carolina family that had served the state, was considering running. Moore had served in the legislature, been active in state Democratic politics, and served as a state district judge. In the six years prior to the campaign he was associated with a major business firm in the west. His associations with the west were significant because of the occasional tradition that governors should rotate between east and west. Moore announced his candidacy for the nomination in late August, the first candidate in the race.

The announcement was followed by much activity by other potential candidates. By the second week in September, Preyer had resigned his judgeship and stated his intention to run. Approximately one week later Bennett publicly confirmed the speculation that he would not be a candidate but instead would support Preyer.

All of this activity occurred within the context of the fact that the losing candidate in the 1960 runoff primary would likely run again. I. Beverly Lake, a conservative lawyer from Wake Forest, was considered a sure contestant in the 1964 race. Deliberations of other candidates were influenced by the fact that once again conservative Democrats would have a very capable spokesman competing for the nomination. Some political leaders tried to persuade Lake not to enter the contest, but their efforts were not successful and in the fall Lake, the last of the major candidates, entered his name for consideration.

Thus, by January, 1964, North Carolina Democrats knew who the major candidates would be. The filing deadline was still two-and-a-half months away. The primary election was five months away. But the contestants had entered the ring, and the battle was on. The longest primary contest in the state's history had taken shape, and the campaigning had an early start.

A congressional primary contest may develop in a quite different manner. An example is the 5th congressional district Democratic nomination in 1966. The incumbent announced in mid-1965 that he would not seek re-election. He retired because he was tired. Immediately the incumbent's legislative assistant made public his decision to be a candidate for the congressional seat. No more formal announcements were forthcoming until in February, 1966. However, private meetings and public speculation were evident throughout the winter. Formal announcements were held up by the fact that the state's congressional districts were being redrawn by the state legislature, and the new plan had to meet the approval of a federal court. The court gave its temporary approval of the plan in the third week of February. At the beginning of the next week a second candidate announced his intentions. Approximately three weeks later a third candidate revealed his plans. The last candidate officially entered the race by mid-March. Pre-announcement maneuvering took place from December to March with approximately three months remaining before the primary election.

The two illustrations should not be considered typical. They are included to indicate factors that play a part in determining the length of a campaign.

In future years primary campaigns can be expected to start earlier although not necessarily last longer. The 1967 General Assembly moved the first primary election from the last Saturday to the first Saturday in May.

The campaign calendar for the general election also varies, but activity generally becomes most intense beginning in September. The activity continues until voting booths close on election day. From the announcement of candidacy for the nomination to the general election of

1964, the Democratic gubernatorial nominee spent fourteen months seeking votes and the Republican nominee spent nine months.

The importance of reviewing the schedule of political events lies in a desire to understand the campaign as a political process. American political campaigns are quite extended and possibly prolonged. Whether they are too long is debatable. But throughout the period much organization and activity takes place. We now proceed to these subjects.

Campaign Organization.   Frequently campaigns for party nominations will be personal organizations. The political party organization is expected to remain neutral in such contests and generally does. These personal organizations for major offices will include a campaign manager, a publicity man, research staff, clerical personnel, and many workers who do a great variety of tasks. The organization of general election campaigns will be similar except that the party organization generally throws its full strength into the battle. Frequently the candidate's personal organizations and party organization are identical.

Campaign organization for a statewide office will be used to illustrate this aspect of politics. In a campaign for an important statewide office the organization is usually coordinated from a state headquarters with subordinate units located at local levels. The headquarters is responsible for strategy, planning and scheduling, research and writing, publicity, and supporting activities. These activities are directed and coordinated by a campaign manager who is chosen by the candidate. Other major officials in the headquarters may be a finance chairman and publicity chairman. The responsibilities of these two persons are indicated by their titles. Their importance is highlighted by the specificity of their concerns.

The financial organization is frequently handled independently of the regular organization. The major responsibility of the financial organization, which may have county units, is to secure sufficient funds to support the candidate's activities. In accepting this responsibility, the finance chairman and his subordinates relieve the candidate and other organizations of a major burden.

Publicity is also handled by a major figure in the campaign but is more integrated into the regular organization. The publicity chairman has responsibility for all advertising, communications, and research for the candidate and campaign. For example, newspaper advertisements and articles, television appearances and advertisements, radio spot announcements, billboards, leaflets, posters, and other forms of publicity are directed by this person and his staff. Additional activities include research for speeches and press releases. In recent years publicity has been assigned to public relations firms and/or professional employees with communications expertise. Another frequent activity has been the use of public opinion polls to assist in the campaign.

Clerical staff including secretaries, typists, telephone operators, receptionists, and general workers will be included among headquarters personnel. These generally serve under the direction of the office manager. Other types of services may be used by a campaign organization, but those previously mentioned are most common and indispensable.

Work by the state organization is frequently complemented by activities at subordinate levels. In a statewide campaign, for example, county units are created to assist at the local levels. These local organizations generally follow the plan used in the state headquarters except that fewer people and less bureaucratization are very likely. Circumstances of the local political climate will have a considerable impact on the nature of such organizations.

Campaigns for offices that have constituencies smaller than the state may not have an organization that explicitly provides for all the needs and services discussed previously. The level and type of organization will be influenced considerably by the office being sought and the structure of competition that characterizes the office. Obviously campaign organization of an incumbent officeholder who faces only token opposition will differ significantly from that of a person competing intensely with others for the same office. But when a contest does occur, organization is vital to all contestants. Whether that organization is highly bureaucratized or rather informal, it will have an impact on the outcome.

In general, campaign organization at any level is charged with several major functions. Most important is planning the campaign and coordinating all activities that contribute to the campaign's effort. Second is communicating to the people the candidate or party and its program as effectively as is possible. Third, the organization must secure workers to carry out the plans and to assist in communications. Next, there is at some place in the organization a group responsible for finances. Obviously little could be done without sufficient resources. Finally, the organization must see to it that its work is brought to a culmination by special election day activities. Chief among the objectives is to get enough of the right voters to the polls.

Campaign Activities. A variety of activities can contribute to the objective of winning the election. It can be said without fear of contradiction that all have been tried. Campaigning is not restricted to, indeed it is not dominated by, activities that will fully inform the voter and assist him in making a rational decision. Campaigning involves selling a candidate, and this may be done through emotional as well as intellectual persuasion.

Most important is to get the people acquainted with the candidate. Much time, effort, and resources are devoted to achieving what is called "name familiarity." If a candidate can get the public to recognize who he is and what office he is seeking, he has made considerable achievement. This is why communications are basic to campaigning. Newspaper advertisements, television spots, billboards, and other forms of publicity are used to familiarize the public with the candidate. These devices frequently do not tell voters about the issues or programs except in very abbreviated fashion. But that does not diminish their importance.

Personal exposure is also significant in campaigning. Candidates attempt to see as many people and visit as many places as possible. In county-by-county tours, by campaign rallies, barbecues, fish frys, brunswick stew suppers, chicken dinners, and through other means the candidate can see and talk to a large number of people. These mass participation activities supplement the trips through the office, to the factory gate, to the shopping center, to the downtown district, and others that involve handshaking and a few select words to individual voters.

Additional campaign speeches before general audiences, civic clubs, neighborhood teas, or special meetings provide opportunities for the candidate to discuss his complete program or examine particular parts of it which are of interest to a specific audience. Such meetings also provide opportunities for candidates to field questions from individuals in the audience. Properly handled, this type of candidate-voter exchange can reap benefits for the candidate.

The many activities of the campaign can provide publicity for the candidate; when he is doing something that is news, an efficient publicity staff will provide news releases reporting his travels, meetings, speeches, and other activities.

The campaign organization can do much on the candidate's behalf without his being actively involved. Auxiliary organizations in support of the candidate are frequently formed. Doctors for Smith, Businessmen for Jones, Students for Brown are hypothetical examples. Such groups are formed by prominent persons who have given their support. These organizations are usually letterhead groups that engage in mass mailings and publicity. The headquarters may also mail brochures about the candidate's career, family, and program in the hope of reaching people who do not take an active part in the campaign. Telephone campaigns may bring a personal message on behalf of the candidate to every voter in the district. Finally, the existence of a campaign headquarters in a convenient location provides a place for interested citizens to congregate and exchange ideas over light refreshments—compliments of the candidate.

The culmination of the long campaign and the varied activities is the work on election day to get out the right voters in sufficient numbers. Transporting voters to the polls, providing baby-sitting services, placing someone at the polls to greet voters, making last-minute sales talks, designating poll watchers—all of these are standard activities for election day. What is not done before or on this day must merely be a lesson for future campaigns and contests.

Campaign Finance. An aspect of campaigning regulated in North Carolina and many other states is campaign finance. Financing political activities is a major part of any effort to seek public office. Because it is basic, finance is controlled, or at least an attempt is made to control it.[2]

The North Carolina statutes that regulate political finance have as their principal objective the disclosure of receipts and expenditures in elections. Candidates must report expenditures and contributions that are known to them and that occur in primary elections. No state law requires reporting by candidates in general elections. North Carolina is one of six states that excepts candidates' reports in general elections. However, the state does require all committees organized for candidates and parties to report in all primary, general, and special elections. Federal laws require reporting of various aspects of financing campaigns for candidates to each house of the United States Congress. Disclosure permits publicity thought to aid in regulating activities.

Depending on the type of election, every candidate for public office and every committee organized for the benefit of a candidate must report all contributions made to them and all disbursements made by them or for their benefit. Candidates for all federal, state, and district offices must report to the secretary of state. Candidates for other offices file their reports with the Superior Court in the county where they reside. The contents of the report are specified by law. The name and address of each contributor, amount and date of each contribution, and the sum of all contribu-

2. Major references for this section include: State Board of Elections, *Election Laws of the State of North Carolina, 1966* (Raleigh, N.C., 1966); and Henry W. Lewis, *Primary and General Election Law and Procedure—1966* (Chapel Hill, N.C.: Institute of Government, 1966).

tions must be reported. In a similar manner, the precise expenditures must be listed. The disbursements report must include the name and address of each person receiving money; the amount, date, and purpose of each expenditure; the same information on all "reported" expenditures; and the total of all expenditures.

Reports are to be filed at two times. A preliminary report is due ten days before the election. A final report covering the entire campaign must be made twenty days after the election. Requiring a report during the campaign can influence the political contest. This would be particularly true if the resources and expenditures of the contestants were disclosed as unequal. Money could, and in all likelihood would, become an issue in the campaign.

North Carolina does not follow the practice of some states and the federal government by putting limits on individual contributions and on the total expenditures. Many of the limits have been found to be unrealistic. Furthermore, they can be circumvented by taking advantage of the loopholes in the laws. In 1962 the President's Commission on Campaign Cost recommended that the limits of contributions and expenditures be abolished.

Sources of campaign funds are not regulated in this state in the same manner as in many states. The law prohibits corporations and insurance companies from contributing to political campaigns. There are no limitations put on solicitations from or contributions by labor unions and public employees.

In 1964 several Republican candidates charged during the election that the state commissioner of motor vehicles was improperly soliciting funds from state employees, including members of the highway patrol. The commissioner admitted the action but said it was not improper. He was supported by the governor. A violation of federal law prohibiting a state official from such action if the department uses federal funds was claimed, and removal of the official was requested. The controversy brought attention to action that may occur frequently when state employees are not protected by state law. But an investigation by federal authorities determined that the department did not come under the act because it was not receiving federal funds. Subsequent to the election, report became public that a law restricting such means of fund-raising would be considered in the legislature. However, no action has been taken to improve the situation.

Laws regulating political finance in North Carolina are similar to laws of other states and to federal legislation in that these laws have not succeeded in providing effective restrictions on the resources and distribution of political money. Enforcement is difficult and lacking, and there has been little success in securing full disclosure of financial activities. However, more conscientious and realistic drafting of the laws would assist greatly in providing an aura of respect for the law that would partially relieve the difficulties of enforcement and achieve a more accurate and complete record of activities.

Because of the inadequacies and imprecision of the laws, it is difficult, if not impossible, to set forth a typical case of campaign finances—both contributions and expenditures. The subject of political finance at the national level has only recently been subject to systematic investigation. Attention to the subject on state and local levels has not been very great. Despite the difficulty in securing reliable information, several examples of finance will be illustrative.

The major political activity at the state level is the campaign for the Democratic gubernatorial nomination and the general election for that office. In 1964 a very prolonged and heated primary contest took place. It involved three major candidates and took two primaries to settle. Expenses reported for the primary campaign were as follows:[3]

	Contributions	Expenditures
Lake (1st primary)	$ 96,109.83	$103,495.57
Moore (1st primary)	129,184.50	128,735.26
Preyer (1st primary)	104,859.00	113,984.00
Moore (2nd primary)	70,231.37	96,109.30
Preyer (2nd primary)	35,661.59	44,610.50

This primary contest involved a total of $436,046 in contributions and $486,935 in expenditures. On the basis of these figures the expenditure by all three candidates for each vote cast was $.46 in the first primary and $.18 in the runoff election.

It is obvious that this political contest attracted much money. The campaign chests of the three candidates in the first primary were roughly equal. The person who reported spending the most money did not receive the largest number of votes; however, the candidate who spent the smallest amount received the fewest votes, but the amount of money involved is not related to the number of votes received. In the second primary the available resources were not even. In fact, one candidate received almost twice as much as the other and his expenditure more than doubled that of his losing opponent. Apparently the losing candidate had difficulty in attracting contributions to his cause. Although there are differences in the amounts received and spent, one common feature also appears in the figures: all candidates report deficits. In no case does a candidate report receiving as much as he spent.

3. Based on reports filed in the Office of the Secretary of State.

The largest deficit is reported by the candidate who won.

Costs of the general election contest as reported indicate that it was not as expensive as the primary. Figures used for the general election are those reported by the candidates and/or the state party. Not all the money spent by the state organization was used for the gubernatorial campaign. Expenses were also incurred in contests for other executive offices, legislative offices, and judicial offices. For example, the state party headquarters frequently donates money to the party congressional nominees, particularly when their chances of winning are great. Finances reported are as follows:

	Contributions	Expenditures
Gavin for Governor	$ 48,155.05	$ 48,148.93
State Republican Party	97,208.90	96,893.78
	145,363.95	145,042.71
State Democratic Party	106,288.66	95,255.01
Bank Loans		50,000.00
		145,225.01
Deficit		38,936.35

The two parties had expenditures of almost equal amounts if the outstanding bank loans of the Democratic party totaling $50,000 are considered in this category. However, the Republicans received more than they spent, while the Democrats finished the campaign with a substantial deficit. The Republican party had enough funds and not enough votes, while the Democrats found themselves with more votes but insufficient funds. In this election the total amount spent by the two parties averaged about $.21 per vote. This figure is considerably below the per-vote costs in the Democratic primary.

A more systematic examination of campaign finance can be secured by looking at congressional elections in 1960, 1962, 1964, and 1966.[4] The examination is based on figures reported to the Clerk of the United States House of Representatives in accordance with federal law. This law requires a candidate to report all contributions and expenditures made by him or "with his knowledge or consent." Frequently candidates take the position that committees and organizations created on their behalf handle most of their financing without their knowledge or consent. Furthermore, committees that operate in a single state are not required to report, according to the law. Thus major loopholes exist. Reports of contributions and expenditures may exclude major financial facts of the several campaigns. Evidence of the incompleteness of the federal reports for some campaigns is that state reports that do include committee activities frequently differ from those filed with the House Clerk.

Table 6 provides basic figures for the costs of congressional campaigns in the state. Several features of campaign finance are apparent from the data. The reported costs of congressional campaigns have been increasing over the period, and the amount of contributions has also gone up. However, while in 1960 there was a major difference between receipts and expenditures, by 1966 the difference had decreased considerably. But in all years more money was reported spent than received. Over the period both parties reported more expenses than contributions. On these reports the Republican and Democratic parties' records at balancing their reports are about equal.

4. Based on reports filed with the appropriate congressional officers and reported in *Congressional Quarterly Weekly Reports,* June 30, 1961; June 26, 1963; January 21, 1966; and August 11, 1967 (Washington, D.C.: Congressional Quarterly, Inc.).

Table 6   Campaign Finances in North Carolina Congressional Elections, 1960-66

Year	Total Receipts		Total Expenditures	
	Democrat	Republican	Democrat	Republican
1960	$ 15,678 (32%)	$33,439 (68%)	$ 21,171 (29%)	$52,330 (71%)
1962	35,553 (40%)	52,820 (60%)	39,386 (38%)	64,030 (62%)
1964	46,691 (44%)	59,741 (56%)	52,557 (46%)	62,395 (54%)
1966	121,734 (64%)	68,252 (36%)	138,183 (65%)	73,545 (35%)

Sources: *Congressional Quarterly Weekly Reports*, June 30, 1961; June 26, 1963; January 21, 1966; and August 11, 1967 (Washington, D.C.: Congressional Quarterly, Inc.).

But the campaign chests and costs are not equal. Except in 1966, Republican candidates reported total receipts and expenditures which are greater than those of the Democratic candidates. While the record varies from one district to another across the state, Republicans as a group have more money to spend. However, data indicate that they are losing their advantage. The 1960 figures indicate that the state's minority party accounted for more than two-thirds of the receipts and expenditures. By 1964 their margin had decreased to slightly more than one-half of the reported funds. In 1966, Republicans received and spent about one-third of the money used in congressional elections. A look at individual district contests reveals a slight variation from the statewide picture. In 1960 Republicans reported larger expenditures in ten of twelve contests and in 1962, seven of eight contests. By 1964 and again in 1966 Democratic candidates spent more in six of ten contests.

The range of expenditures by candidates is considerable. In an uncontested election, the costs of campaigning are limited to the filing fee, between $225 and $300. When candidates from each party are appealing to the voters, the costs rise. The costliest campaigns in each year except 1966 have been on behalf of Republican candidates. In 1960 that party's candidate reported a high expenditure of $16,400; in 1962, $26,155; in 1964, $27,350; and in 1966, $21,174. The most expensive Democratic campaigns during the period were $8,650; $15,224; $15,476; and $57,660. Most campaigns did not involve amounts of this magnitude. Taking the combined expenditures for the two candidates, the mean and median costs of contested congressional campaigns in each year is as follows:

	Mean	Median
1960	$ 3,462	$ 6,208
1962	8,469	13,133
1964	4,399	12,636
1966	16,822	23,380

The two sets of figures indicate that reported costs have risen substantially during this decade.

Table 7   Contributions of $500 or More in North Carolina Congressional Campaigns, 1960-66

Year	Total amount of gifts $500 or more	Total amount as percentage of all gifts	Percentage Democratic gifts from $500 or more	Percentage Republican gifts from $500 or more	Percentage of gifts $500 or more from committees
1960	$31,622	64.3	71.0	83.0	63.7
1962	48,030	53.7	64.5	46.5	63.3
1964	80,529	75.0	56.9	90.2	65.0
1966	99,698	52.4	44.8	66.0	71.2

Sources: *Congressional Quarterly Weekly Reports,* June 30, 1961, June 26, 1963; January 21, 1966; and August 11, 1967 (Washington, D.C.: Congressional Quarterly, Inc.).

Variations exist not only in amounts available and amounts spent but also in the sources from which money is received. Table 7 looks at the place of large gifts ($500 or more) in the financial picture of congressional campaigns. In the years covered, the large contributions have provided from about one-half to three-fourths of the funds reported. Both parties depend on such gifts from relatively few contributors for a major part of the money. This dependence varies from a high of 90 per cent for the Republicans in 1964 to a low of 45 per cent for the Democratic party in the most recent election. The Democratic dependence shows more of a pattern. Since 1960 Democrats have relied decreasingly on gifts of $500 or more. Gifts of this size come from two kinds of contributors: individuals and committees. In the years reported, almost two-thirds of the money contributed came from committees. Most of the committees are organized at various levels by the political parties to raise and distribute money. Among committees that are frequent contributors to congressional campaigns are the Democratic and Republican National committees, the Republican Congressional Boosters Club, the Democratic and Republican Congressional Campaign committees, the Democratic and Republican state executive committees, and local committees organized on behalf of particular candidates or parties.

Financing nominations and campaigns of candidates for offices such as state legislator usually involves less money and depends upon personal and local resources. It is very unusual for such campaigns to cost over $2,000. Of course, if the district is large both in size and population and the contest intense, the cost of campaigning may increase.

Elections

Statewide elections for governor, lieutenant governor, and other executive officials in North Carolina are held every four years. These elections occur at the same time as the national election of the President. They are held on the first Tuesday after the first Monday in November. United States congressmen and state senators and representatives are elected every two years. Municipal elections may or may not be held at the same time depending on local laws.

Regulation of Elections. Elections are regulated and administered by state and county election boards. These groups are generally responsible for the conduct and supervision of the election process.

The State Board of Elections is composed of five persons appointed by the governor.[5] No more than three of the persons may come from a single party. This means that the majority is always from the governor's party. North Carolina's board has had three Democrats and two Republicans from its inception. Appointments are for four-year terms. The members elect their own chairman. The chairman is a man from the majority party who has been designated as the governor's choice. The board has an office in the state capitol and a staff that includes full-time professional and clerical employees headed by an executive secretary.

The state board has authority to appoint the county boards of elections which have three members. No more than two of the members may be from the same political party. Appointments are made on the basis of nominations received from the state chairmen of political parties. That is, the Democratic and Republican chairmen file a list of three persons from each county and the local board members must be selected from this list. Once again, this procedure results in all one hundred county boards having two members from the Democratic party and one from the Republican party. This is true even in counties where Republicans frequently receive a majority of the votes. County board members serve two-year terms and may be

5. Major sources on the conduct of elections include: State Board of Elections, *Election Laws in North Carolina, 1966* (Raleigh, N.C.: 1966); and Henry W. Lewis, *Primary and General Election Law and Procedure—1966* (Chapel Hill, N.C.: Institute of Government, 1966).

reappointed. The chairman is selected by and from the members.

All matters pertaining to the execution of election laws and administration of election machinery are the responsibilities of the state and local election boards. Among these are the following: appointing of election officials including registrars, judges, and clerks for the several precincts; establishing precincts; registering voters; hearing challenges; printing and distributing ballots; supervising the election; counting the ballots; certifying the results; and issuing results of the election.

Ultimate authority for the conduct of elections rests with the State Board of Elections. This group may investigate irregularities and remove persons from office. It also makes recommendations for legislation to the General Assembly.

Although occasional irregularities do occur, the general record of the administration of election laws in this state has been superior to that of other states in the region. When questions do arise, the state board is usually quick to investigate and maintain a record of fair administration of elections. The abuse of absentee balloting has been a particularly bothersome problem in the state.

Ballots and Balloting.   Most voting in the state is done by paper ballots, although some locales have adopted voting machines for the purpose. In the general election of 1966 fewer than twenty counties used machines. All ballots, whether paper or machine, are party-column. That is, the names of candidates are listed by party. In addition, provision is made at the head of each party column for straight-ticket voting in general elections. A voter, by properly marking the ballot at the top of the column, may vote for all candidates in the column.

Different ballots, almost identical in form, are used for the several levels of government. Separate ballots include party nominees for President and Vice President, and United States Senate and House of Representatives. Others include lists of nominees for state offices, county offices, township offices, and constitutional amendments. Appropriate adaptations are made for primary ballots.

Write-ins are permitted in general elections except for President and Vice President, but not in primaries. While no lines are provided for writing names on the ballot, space is left that can be used for this purpose.

Polling places are secured by the county boards of elections and must be properly publicized. Often the places will be public buildings, but some private establishments are used. Schools, fire stations, court houses, and other public buildings are most frequently used. However, filling stations, country stores, and privately owned dwellings are also used.

Voting places are manned by precinct registrars and judges appointed by the county boards of nominations made by party county chairmen. Registrars and judges receive the voters, determine that they are properly registered to vote, and distribute appropriate ballots. These officials are immediately responsible for elections in a particular polling place. Each party and independent candidate may appoint poll watchers and observers to represent them in the precinct. Such persons are not election officials but must be approved by the precinct officials.

Normally, voting must be done in person at the appropriate precinct. However, in statewide general elections absentee voting by civilians is permitted if the person is to be absent from the county where he normally votes or is physically unable to go to the polls.

Applications for and issuance of absentee ballots is the responsibility of the chairman of the county board of elections. Applications in cases of absence from the county can be filed from forty-five to six days before the elections. Applications must be properly completed under oath administered by a duly qualified officer. Upon receiving the application, the chairman must receive approval of a majority of the county board before he can issue the ballot. Delivery of the ballots to the voter is done by the chairman. The ballot is to be marked in the presence of an officer with a seal who is authorized to administer oaths, i.e., notary public and clerk of the superior court. Ballots must be received by the chairman no later than noon on the Saturday before the election. These regulations apply to civilian persons.

Individuals in the armed forces and "service-connected civilians" may apply for absentee ballots to the secretary of state or the chairman of the county board of elections. In either case the county chairman processes the application and issues the absentee ballot. A limited group of persons specified by law can register and vote in primaries by absentee applications.

All applications for and filing of absentee ballots are regulated by quite precise and elaborate provisions.[6] The administration of such regulations and the use of absentee voting, especially by civilians, has been the subject of considerable controversy.

Ballots are counted by the precinct officials, and returns from each precinct are filed with the County Board of Elections. Publication of vote totals is handled by the county board. A county canvass of all precinct results is held on

6. Because of the complexity of these regulations, voters should consult appropriate officials to determine their individual eligibility and procedure.

the second day after the election. At this time the official vote is determined. If disputes or questions arise regarding results, the county board can determine what action is necessary. For statewide elections, the State Board of Elections conducts a canvass approximately three weeks after the election.

CHAPTER FOUR ⊠

INTRAPARTY COMPETITION

A major preoccupation of political parties is to win public office so that they can make decisions that are necessary in a political system. But before party candidates can take office, a more important decision must be made by the electorate. The electorate must pull levers and mark ballots to record individual decisions. The product of these separate decisions is the ultimate decision of which persons and parties will be entrusted with political power. So in elections, the people and the parties meet.

In this chapter, we will review these meetings over the last quarter of the present century. The focus is on nominating choices and intraparty competition. The internal battles of the Democratic and Republican parties that were decided in nominating primaries are examined for the period 1940-1966. In the next chapter interparty competition between Democrats and Republicans will be reviewed. Our concern will be with contests for President, state executive offices, the United States Senate and House of Representatives, and the North Carolina General Assembly. Our objective is to reveal patterns of political competition in North Carolina.

Presidential Nominations
North Carolina does not hold a presidential preference primary. Both parties select their delegates to the quadrennial national conventions by state conventions. There is no statutory requirement for instructed delegations. Thus the

delegates can go to the convention uninhibited or at least uninstructed in their voting preferences.

In the period 1940-66, the Democratic and Republican parties held seven national conventions. Four of the seven Democratic conventions were essentially confirmations of incumbent Presidents' bids for renomination. In 1940 and 1944 North Carolina's delegations supported the incumbent President, Franklin Roosevelt, by casting all the convention votes for him. The same was true in 1964 when Lyndon Johnson was nominated after having served as President for the last year of John Kennedy's term. But in 1948 the state's delegation did not go along with President Harry Truman's bid for renomination. Instead, North Carolina cast nineteen of its thirty-two votes for a fellow southerner, Senator Richard Russell of Georgia. The other thirteen votes did go to President Truman.

During the period, there were three conventions in which the choice did not involve an incumbent President and was not clearly evident before the convention voted on the nominee. The conventions were in 1952, 1956, and 1960. In the first of these, the North Carolina Democratic delegation gave an overwhelming majority of its votes (an average of twenty-five out of thirty-two on the three ballots) to Senator Russell, as once again the South showed its strength in the party. The eventual nominee, Adlai Stevenson, did receive about one-fifth of the state's votes. In 1956 the delegation indicated that it was ready to accept Stevenson by casting thirty-four and one-half of thirty-six votes for the party's nominee. The most recent contested presidential nomination was in 1960. Once again North Carolina showed its inclination for a southerner. The state's votes were divided among the four candidates as follows: Lyndon Johnson, twenty-seven and one-half; John Kennedy, six; Stuart Symington, three; and George Smathers, one-half.

The record of votes cast by North Carolina's delegations to the Democratic national conventions indicates that the state party's representatives have usually been in significant agreement on a nominee but that they have varied in the kind of person they support. Only once (1948) was the delegation greatly divided over the nominee. On three occasions they cast votes for incumbent Presidents and on three occasions for a favorite son from the South. The party's record in supporting the eventual winner when no clear choice was evident is very poor. In three of the four conventions in which there was a contest, North Carolina's delegation supported the losing candidate, and in all three conventions the delegations were supporting the more conservative front-running candidates.

Only once in the last quarter-century was the Republican nominee for President an incumbent. North Carolina supported President Dwight Eisenhower in 1956 in his request for renomination. In 1960, North Carolina supported the Republican Vice President, Richard Nixon, as did all other state delegations, except one. In the other five Republican national conventions the decision was not as certain, and this is manifest in the vote of North Carolina delegations.

In 1940 the convention was split among several candidates and so was the state's delegation. The three major contenders were Thomas Dewey of New York, Robert Taft of Ohio, and Wendell Wilkie of Indiana. On the first ballot the state delegation gave Dewey the largest vote (nine of twenty-three), but not a majority. Taft received seven votes, the second highest number. By the third ballot Dewey lost strength, but the choice still was not clear. By the fifth ballot only Taft and Wilkie were left, and the delegation gave Wilkie a one-vote margin. On the sixth and final ballot Wilkie gained and Taft declined, but the winning nominee received only fifteen of the state's votes. In 1944 the state delegation was unanimous in supporting the convention's choice, Thomas Dewey.

The 1948 convention saw the return of Taft and Dewey, with Harold Stassen of Minnesota being the third major contender. Throughout the convention voting, Dewey received the majority of the state's votes, but this amounted to only sixteen of twenty-three on the first ballot and seventeen on the second. The remainder of the delegation was divided among several other candidates. By the third ballot Dewey received all this state's votes and the convention majority.

The delegation to the 1952 convention was initially split between the two leading contenders, Dwight Eisenhower and Robert Taft. Taft won fourteen of twenty-six votes on the first ballot. By the second ballot North Carolina Republicans threw all of their support to Eisenhower; the other delegates supported him too, and the General was nominated. In 1964 the Republican convention was divided among several candidates, but the state's delegation was not. Its unanimous choice was Senator Barry Goldwater, the convention's nominee.

In the seven Republican conventions since 1940, North Carolina's delegation has been either solidly in support of one candidate or it has divided sharply between candidates. In two of the contests (1940 and 1952) its initial support was given to candidates who eventually lost the nomination. There has been no particular consistency in the political orientation of the state's Republican choice. Sometimes the choice was the conservative candidate; at other times the moderates won their favor. But in all seven conventions the state's Republicans tested the political winds, and ended up voting for the convention's choice.

Intraparty Competition: Democrats

Executive Offices. There are ten executive offices which are popularly elected in North Carolina. These include governor; lieutenant governor; attorney general; secretary of state; treasurer; auditor; superintendent of public instruction; and commissioners of insurance, labor, and agriculture. The last seven are designated as the council of state. Competition within the Democratic party for these offices takes place in the party's nominating primary. The Democrats have used primaries throughout this period; when they were the clear majority party, the primary was the most significant election, because its nominee would be virtually assured of election in the November balloting.

Several sets of data will be used to picture competition within the Democratic party. The frequency of primaries, number of primary contestants, the division of the vote, the necessity of a runoff primary, and the presence of incumbents are used to indicate the level of competition. Table 8 provides the details. Data on the number of contestants for the Democratic nomination make it quite clear that the party's internal competition is focused on the highest state offices—governor and lieutenant governor. While there is variation from one office to another and from one election to the next, the pattern of competition is quite evident.

GOVERNOR AND LIEUTENANT GOVERNOR. Attention in the Democratic primary is focused on the gubernatorial nomination. This fact is supported by data on the number

Table 8   Primary Competition for Democratic Nominations to State Executive Offices, 1940-64

Office	Number of nominations[1]	Number of contested primaries	Number of contested primaries involving incumbents	Average number of candidates	Average number of candidates receiving 20% or more	Average per cent of vote received by two highest candidates	Number of runoff primaries	Average vote received by nominee
Governor	7	7	1	4	2	83.0	3	56.9
Lieutenant Governor	7	7	0	3	2	79.7	1	50.4
Attorney General	7	0	–	–	–	–	–	–
Secretary of State	7	3	3	2	2	100.0	0	72.6
Auditor	7	3	3	2	2	100.0	0	68.9
Treasurer	8	3	2	2	2	98.3	0	68.2
Superintendent of Public Instruction	7	0	–	–	–	–	–	–
Commissioner of Agriculture	7	2	2	2	2	100.0	0	70.3
Commissioner of Insurance	8	6	6	2	2	97.6	0	69.3
Commissioner of Labor	7	3	3	3	2	86.0	0	57.5

1. There were seven regular elections during the period. Number varies because of special elections held for unexpired terms.
Sources: Based on data reported in the appropriate volumes of the *North Carolina Manual.*

of competitors, the level of support gained by contestants, and the likelihood of a runoff or second primary. It is not unexpected since this is the biggest prize in the state's political game even though power in the executive branch is significantly diffused among the long list of independently elected officials.

The number of competitors for the Democratic gubernatorial nomination has ranged from a high of seven (1940) to a low of three (1944, 1952). The average number is four. However, it is widely recognized that among those who file for the office, there are some publicity seekers or, at least, less-than-serious contenders. The latter point is substantiated by looking at the number of participants who received a considerable number of votes. If we consider as major or serious contenders only those candidates who received 20 per cent or more of the vote (a generous but not unreasonable standard), the range would be reduced from one to three, with the average reduced to two. It must be recognized that this quantitative determination of major candidates does have its faults. Other measures would produce different results.

A consequence of the number of contestants is the division of votes cast. It is interesting to note that, even though there have been primary contests involving what would be considered many candidates, there has not been a significant fragmentation of the Democratic primary vote. This statement is partially substantiated by the fact that in the seven contests studied, the combined strength of the top three candidates has averaged 91 per cent, and the top two contenders have averaged 83 per cent of the total votes cast.

While these figures do indicate a lack of substantial fragmentation of the party's electorate, they also highlight the fact that a candidate seldom is nominated without a battle. Luther Hodges, who ran for renomination in 1956, is, of course, an exception. He is also the only person to run for governor as an incumbent. Hodges was elected as lieutenant governor in 1952 and succeeded to the higher post at the death of Governor William Umstead in 1954. Hodges received a large vote (86 per cent), even though there were three other candidates. Two other Democratic candidates have been nominated in the first primary with a majority of the votes. In 1944, R. Gregg Cherry received 57 per cent of the vote, and in 1952, Umstead polled 52 per cent. In 1940, with seven contenders for the nomination, J. Melville Broughton was nominated in the first primary with less than one-third of the votes (31 per cent). It is amazing that such a small percentage could make this decision. Thus, four of the seven Democratic gubernatorial nominees were chosen in the first primary, but only two received substantial support.

There were three campaigns for the party's nominations during this period that required a second primary: the contests of 1948, 1960, and 1964. In 1948 and 1964, vote totals of the top two candidates were very close. In both cases the candidate who led the first primary was defeated in the runoff. Kerr Scott and Dan Moore each defeated the leader of the first primary. In 1960, when Sanford and Lake were major contenders, the former won substantially in both the first and second primaries.

The structure of competition in the Democratic party as illustrated by contests for the gubernatorial nomination may be characterized as one that avoids both fragmentation and simple ratification of the front runner and clear choice. Competition does exist but is restrained. V. O. Key suggests that a factor of great significance in the development of the structure is the existence of significant support for the Republican party.[1] We will return to this subject subsequently.

The office of lieutenant governor in North Carolina has generally not attracted a great amount of attention. The lieutenant governor is designated by the Constitution to serve as president of the Senate and to succeed to the office of governor if the incumbent dies or resigns. This officer is not a member of the governor's council of state, and he may well not be among the governor's intimate advisers. In fact, it is possible that the lieutenant governor on occasion could be suspected of aspiring to the governorship and conceivably could use his office to attract attention and become a recognized figure in state government. Frequently, the race for lieutenant governor is unrelated to that of the gubernatorial contestants. It may be of mutual interest for the party's nominees for these two offices not to become too closely associated and identified with one another.

With these ideas in mind about the position, we can better understand the structure of competition that surrounds the position. The number of contestants for the Democratic nomination during this period has been rather stable. It has ranged from two to five, with an average of three. The average number of contestants who received more than 20 per cent of the total vote is two. In all but one case the party's nominee was selected in the first primary. In these six cases only two of the winners received a majority vote. In other words, four of the state's last seven lieutenant governors were nominated by less than a majority of the participating electorate.

The most recent contest for the Democratic nomination

1. V. O. Key, Jr., *Southern Politics* (New York: Random House, nc., 1949), p. 223.

to this office was close and required a runoff primary. There were three candidates; only two, however, were considered strong enough contenders to win the nomination. The results of the runoff primary indicate the strength of the contestants. Robert W. Scott won by 14,000 votes out of a total of 732,000 votes.

No nominee of the Democratic party for governor or lieutenant governor has been nominated without opposition. Aspiring candidates have always had to fight for the right to carry the party's banner and head the party's slate in the state.

OTHER EXECUTIVE OFFICES. Consistently, Democratic party nominations for the other eight executive positions in the state government do not attract many contestants. More than half (54.5 per cent) of the nominations did not involve a primary contest, but some positions were less contested than others. During the period all nominations for the offices of attorney general and superintendent of public instruction were determined without a primary, in that incumbents were the only persons filing for the office from the Democratic party. On the other extreme, the position of commissioner of insurance was uncontested on only two of eight occasions. One-third of the nominations were decided in primaries in which two contestants were contending. Never did more than three persons compete for the nomination to any of these offices. This is in striking contrast to the findings on governor and lieutenant governor nominations. Other features of the structure of competition for these offices are provided in Table 8.

The lack of competition for these offices is also indicated by a look at the votes. In only about one-tenth of the contests did the winning candidate receive less than 61 per cent of the vote. Even if contests in which only one person filed for the nomination are discounted, the results indicate that nominees received about two-thirds of the votes. Once again, variations appear between the various offices. The nominee for the secretary of state received the highest average number of votes in contested primaries over the last quarter century. Nominees for the position of commissioner of labor received the lowest average support. But nominees for none of the offices received average votes which were less than those cast for the two top executive posts. At no time during the period was a second primary necessary to determine the party's nominee.

Frequently, lack of competition for political offices is related to or derives from the fact that an incumbent runs for renomination. This is possible for positions on the council of state and office of attorney general in North Carolina. Persons who occupy these offices can succeed themselves, a political privilege which is not granted to the governor and lieutenant governor. In nineteen of the twenty times when a primary was held during this period incumbents were running. Never was an incumbent defeated in his bid for renomination. Ninety-five per cent of the times when the Democratic party had to select nominees for these eight offices during the past twenty-six years, an incumbent has been renominated. The presence of an incumbent undoubtedly has an influence on the number of contests that are held and the margin of victory that is achieved.

During this period there has been only moderate change in the personnel who have sought the Democratic nominations to these executive offices. The Democratic nominee for secretary of state in each case has been the present incumbent, Thad Eure. No other person has remained in one office at this level for a similar period. For the other six positions the average number of different persons nominated is three and the average tenure as a nominee is nine years. The most frequent change in nominees has been for the position of commissioner of insurance. That is also the office for which there have been the fewest uncontested primaries.

Finally, a review of the competition since 1940 shows contradictory trends in the number of contestants and in the average winning vote. During the earlier half of the period, primaries involved an average of three candidates, and the winning candidate received 70 per cent of the vote. In the last half the number of candidates has decreased to two, and the winning percentage has decreased to 67.

United States Congress: Senate.   In the period 1940-66 there have been twelve Democratic nominations for the office of United States Senator (see Table 9). Twice during that time the Democratic nominee was selected without a contest from a member of his own party. Clyde Hoey in 1950 and Sam Ervin, Jr., in 1962, both incumbents, won their party's nomination without opposition. At other times as few as two and as many as seven persons competed for the party candidacy. The average number of contestants is three. However, in most years only two candidates could attract as much as 20 per cent of the vote. Thus, the party's votes were not scattered among a large number of candidates receiving small fragments of support.

In all contested primaries the candidates receiving the two highest numbers of votes won combined totals of at least 90 per cent. The average for these persons was 97 per cent. This figure indicates the insignificance of the minor candidates. Only once in the period was a second primary necessary. In 1950, a heated first primary occurred between Senator Frank Graham, who had been recently

Table 9 Primary Competition for Democratic Nominations to Congressional Offices, 1940-66

Office	Number of nominations	Number of contested primaries	Number involving incumbents	Average number of candidates	Average number of candidates receiving 20% or more	Average per cent of vote received by two highest candidates	Number of runoff primaries	Average vote received by nominees
U.S. Senate								
Position 1[1]	8	7	7	3.8	2	92.5	1	54.0
Position 2	4	2	2	3.5	1.5	97.6	0	75.5
U.S. House								
District								
1st[2]	15	4	3	3	2	92.5	0	65.9
2nd	14	4	4	2	2	100.0	0	68.4
3rd	14	6	5	3	2	87.2	1	70.2
4th	14	5	5	2	2	99.0	0	67.7
5th	14	12	11	2.5	2	95.1	1	62.6
6th	14	10	9	2	2	95.4	0	64.1
7th	14	7	6	2.5	2	94.2	2	61.0
8th	14	10	7	2	2	98.1	1	61.3
9th	14	2	1	3	2	90.4	1	68.8
10th	14	9	3	2	2	97.5	0	70.3
11th	14	7	3	2.5	2	94.4	2	64.2
12th[3]	10	3	1	4	2	81.3	1	53.3

1. There were four regular contests. Number varies because of special election.
2. There were fourteen regular contests. Number varies because of special election.
3. Existent only from 1942 through 1960.
Sources: Based on data reported in the appropriate volumes of the *North Carolina Manual.*

appointed to the seat, and challenger Willis Smith. Graham received 49 per cent of the vote, but Smith exercised his right to call for a second primary. In that contest, Graham's portion of the vote decreased slightly and Smith won by approximately 20,000 votes, 52 per cent of those cast. On the average, the winners of the first primary and the eventual senatorial nominees have won a healthy two-thirds of the vote (67 per cent).

Every primary for senatorial nominee of the Democratic party since 1942 has included an incumbent. But the incumbents have not always successfully defended their positions. In five of the twelve elections the incumbent has lost in his bid for renomination. These five cases, however, involve only three persons. In 1948 and in 1954 the incumbents, William Umstead and Alton Lennon respectively, were running for both a short-term and regular-term nomination. The other incumbent who lost, Frank Graham, was mentioned previously.

The difficulty that incumbents have had resulted in a high rate of turnover in the occupants of one of these two political positions in the late 1940's and early 1950's. From 1946 to 1958 seven persons served as one of the state's two United States Senators. A pattern developed in which an incumbent died, a successor was appointed, and a challenger would defeat the appointee in his bid for renomination. The line-up looks like this: Josiah Bailey, elected 1930, served until his death in 1946. William Umstead, appointed at death of Bailey, was defeated at the next primary by J. Melville Broughton. Broughton served from January, 1949, until his death in March of the same year. At that time he was succeeded by Frank Graham, who was then president of the consolidated University of North Carolina. Graham was defeated by Willis Smith in

1950. Smith served until his death in June, 1953, when Alton Lennon was appointed.

The state's other position in the Senate has had three occupants since 1940. They were Robert R. Reynolds, who served from 1932 to 1945; Clyde Hoey, who was appointed in 1945 and served until his death in 1954; and Sam J. Ervin, Jr., who was appointed by Governor Umstead to succeed Hoey. Ervin won his party's nomination in the primaries in 1956 and 1962.

If the period is divided in half, some idea can be had of the development of competition for these two offices. In each half the average number of nominations was three; however, the winning margins have increased from an average of 59 per cent before 1953 to an average of 67 per cent after that date. This increase can be attributed partially to the longer tenure and more solid positions of the incumbents who bid for renomination.

United States Congress: House of Representatives. Analyzing competition for congressional offices is complicated by the fact that the districts have changed four times over the twenty-six year period. In 1940 the state had eleven congressmen. After the federal census of that year, the delegation was increased to twelve. It remained that size until the 1960 census when it was reduced to eleven. Redistricting occurred in 1961 after the census and reductions and again in 1966 and 1967 after a district court declared the state's districts did not meet constitutional requirements.

Competition within the Democratic party for congressional nomination has been moderate to weak. During the twenty-six year period primary contests occurred in less than half of the cases. That is, the nomination went to a candidate without opposition in 52 per cent of the cases.

In almost all cases the candidate was an incumbent congressman who was seeking renomination.

But occasionally, incumbent congressmen return to the district and are challenged in their bids for renomination. In 73 per cent of the cases in which a contest for the nomination did occur, an incumbent was one of the contestants. And of the fifty-eight cases in which an incumbent sought renomination in the face of opposition, he was defeated only five times. Thus, the influence of incumbents on the election is dramatic. Presence of an incumbent both decreases the likelihood of a contest and, if a contest does occur, his presence is seldom met by defeat.

Furthermore, the margins by which renomination is won are not slight. Since 1940 the average percentage of support for the nominee when a contest does occur is approximately 66. Two out of three voters are willing to give the incumbent another try for re-election. Furthermore, when a contest does occur, it is generally between the incumbent and a single challenger.

Finally, a second (runoff) primary is seldom necessary in congressional elections. In nine cases the nominee was not selected in the first primary. However, incumbents were involved in six of these runoffs.

This discussion has focused on the districts as a whole. There are variations among them. An examination of these variations is necessary to understand more fully the nature of competition within the Democratic party for congressional nominations. The districts with the least competition within the Democratic party are the First, Second, Third, Fourth, and Ninth. All but the Ninth, which comprises counties in the western Piedmont and the Mountains, are in the eastern section of the state. In each of these districts, the congressman was a strong vote-getter and served long tenure in the House of Representatives. In the First District Herbert Bonner served twenty-four years. In the Second District John Kerr served from 1923 to 1952 and was succeeded by L. H. Fountain who has served since 1952. The Third District incumbent was Graham Barden from 1934 to 1960 and David Henderson since then. Harold Cooley served the Fourth District from 1934 until his defeat for election, not renomination, in 1966. The Ninth District has had two Democratic incumbents since 1940, Robert Doughton (1940-52) and Hugh Alexander (1952-62).

The districts with the most competition for nominations are the Fifth, Eighth, and Tenth, in that order. The first two are upper and lower Piedmont districts, respectively, and the Tenth is located in the western Piedmont and Mountain section. The Democratic contenders in these three districts have changed frequently. In the Fifth District three men have about equally divided the period with their incumbencies (Folger, 1941-48; Chatham, 1948-56; Scott, 1956-66). The Eighth District is very similar (Burgin, 1940-45; Deane, 1946-54; Kitchin, 1956-62). The Tenth District has experienced frequent change in contenders for the Democratic nomination and from 1952 to 1960 it was represented by a strong Republican congressman.

An examination of the progress of electoral competition for these offices since 1940 is instructive. In the 1940's the number of candidates and the winning percentage averaged five and 62 respectively; in 1950's, six and 64; and in 1960's, five and 66. The number of candidates has fluctuated, while the winning percentage has increased slightly but steadily. A greater contrast is found between victory margins in presidential and nonpresidential election years. In the former the victorious candidate polled

61 per cent of the vote, while in off-year elections the winner received 67 per cent. In presidential years the competition is more intense because the campaigns produce a higher political fervor and receive more attention.

General Assembly. State legislative politics in North Carolina is not based on slates. These campaigns are frequently conducted without association at higher levels of political combat. Statewide or regional factions may attempt to recruit and sponsor candidates for these offices, but rarely are such efforts made on a wide scale. State legislative politics can be a vital element in the state's political system. Men chosen individually in these elections will have much to say collectively about the issues of the state. These are the state government's closest link with the people. Competition for these seats is also indicative of the level of competition in the counties, that is, local politics.

In the four elections covered in Table 10, there were slightly more contested primaries for seats in the House of Representatives than in the Senate.[2] Much of this lack of intraparty competition can likely be attributed to the frequency of incumbents running for another term. Almost half of the elections did involve incumbents. Furthermore, incumbents were beaten about one-eighth of the times they were challenged. Even less frequent was the need for a runoff primary. The nominee was almost always selected in the first primary.

Jewell concluded after examining competition for legislative nominations in eight southern states that, by all

2. The data and discussion in this section depend heavily on the research of Malcolm E. Jewell, *Legislative Representation in the Contemporary South* (Durham, N.C.: Duke University Press, 1967), especially Chapter Two.

Table 10 Primary Competition for Democratic Nominations for General Assembly Offices, 1958-64

	Number of nominations	Per cent contested primaries	Per cent involving incumbents	Incumbents defeated as per cent of incumbents running	Per cent with runoff primaries
All districts					
Senate	200	49	47	10	5
House	467	62	49	15	6
Democratic districts only					
Senate	115	52	49	8	3
House	254	63	60	16	9

Source: Adapted from M. Jewell, *Legislative Representation in the Contemporary South,* Chapter 2, Tables 2.1 and 2.11.

measures used, North Carolina had the lowest level of Democratic party competition for these offices (see footnote 2). The level of competition is slightly higher in safe Democratic districts than in districts where Republicans present significant electoral competition. Such safe districts are more likely to be located in rural areas, especially in the eastern and middle sections of the state.

Summary. By using several measures we have examined the structure of competition within the Democratic party for popularly elected executive positions and for the state's representatives in the United States Congress and the

state General Assembly. The discussion reveals that variations exist in the majority party from one office to another
and from one area of the state to another.

Table 11   Primary Competition in Democratic Party for State Executive and Congressional Offices, 1940-66

Office	Per cent of nomi-nations con-tested	Per cent con-tested with incum-bent	Average vote won by two highest candi-dates	Per cent con-tested with runoff primaries	Average per cent won by nominee
Governor, Lieutenant Governor	100.0	7.65	81.3	21.4	53.7
Council of State and Attorney General	36.7	100.0	96.9	0.0	67.8
U.S. Senate	75.0	75.0	96.4	8.3	58.8
U.S. House of Representatives	47.9	73.5	93.8	11.4	64.1

Sources: Based on data reported in the appropriate volumes of the
North Carolina Manual.

It is obvious from Table 11 that the most intense competition surrounds the two top executive offices—governor
and lieutenant governor. Not only is the number of uncontested nominees nil, but also the vote is divided among
more candidates, resulting in a more frequent use of primaries and lower margins of victory for the eventual
nominee. Greater competition for these offices, especially
for governor, is to be expected because of the importance
of the positions. But the summary table points up another
important factor that improves understanding of the competition. This is the inability of these two officials to run
for renomination. It is reasonable to conclude that this one

factor has a considerable impact on competition for these offices.

All other executive positions at the state level, the positions in the United States Congress, and the seats in the state legislature do permit renomination. That is, all office-holders in state politics except the governor and lieutenant governor can succeed themselves. However, slight differences do exist between the various offices. A larger number of congressional nominations are contested in primaries. However, incumbents are more likely to run in primaries for nominations to the executive positions than to the congressional offices. Related to this is the fact that votes cast for the two highest candidates for executive and legislative posts are significantly larger than votes for the two highest executive positions. Furthermore, the nominees win by larger margins. Finally, in congressional nominations more incumbent congressmen are defeated, and a second primary is needed more frequently. This conclusion applies to members of both the United States Senate and the House of Representatives, although not equally.

Competition is greatest for the two highest executive offices and least for the other eight offices in the executive branch. Competition for congressional offices falls between these two extremes, but closer to the latter than the former. With the exception of nominations for governor and lieutenant governor and a few congressional districts, competition within the Democratic party is not very intense. Nominees usually win approximately two-thirds of the primary vote.

Democratic Factionalism. Democratic nominations for political offices in North Carolina are generally not the work of slate makers. That is, the hopefuls for legislative and executive nominations do not run as a team comprising candidates for each nomination. Instead, individuals, with personal organizations and personal followings, seek the party's nominations. However, these comments should not be construed to suggest that there are not personal and political affinities between candidates because, since many of the nominees at any single election have worked together in state and national government as public officials, personal relationships and sympathies must exist. Officially and organizationally, these personal ties are convenient, not contractual.

However, factions have operated in North Carolina politics over the past quarter-century and before, for that matter. The groups have focused their efforts and attentions primarily, although not exclusively, on the gubernatorial nomination of the majority party. Several aspects of factional competition for this nomination deserve attention because of the contribution they can make to an understanding of the state's politics.

Factionalism within the Democratic party is characterized by change and fluidity. The factions that compete for the gubernatorial nomination have not remained the same since 1940. What factions field candidates for the nomination depends on which persons have ambitions to live in the governor's mansion. And when factions compete, lines separating them are not clear and rigid.

The period opens with the "Shelby ring" dominating state politics, having successfully fielded a candidate for the gubernatorial nomination in 1928, 1932, 1936, and 1944.[3] The faction was defeated because of a split in 1940.

3. For an examination of Democratic factionalism in the first three elections see, Elmer L. Puryear, *Democratic Party Dissension in North Carolina, 1928-1936* (Chapel Hill: The University of North Carolina Press, 1962).

By 1948, however, the machine of O. Max Gardner was surprised when its candidate, Charles Johnson, state treasurer since 1932, was defeated by Kerr Scott, who had served as commissioner of agriculture since 1936. The state administration was split by this contest between two executive officials. A second primary was required to resolve the conflict.[4]

In 1952 William B. Umstead, who had served as campaign manager for Governor Cherry in 1944 and had received an appointment to the United States Senate in 1948 from Cherry, ran for his party's gubernatorial nomination. In his bid he revived the hopes of people who had supported Gardner, Ehringhaus, Hoey, and Cherry and dimmed the hopes of what was called the Scott faction. But state politics changed early during his term. Umstead died on November 7, 1954, and Lieutenant Governor Luther Hodges succeeded him. In 1956 Hodges ran for renomination as a popular incumbent and, as might be expected, that dulled the hopes of the opposition. This election may also have served to provide a period during which the fever of political factions was allowed to cool. Hodges received 86 per cent of the vote, and three other candidates got token support.

By 1960 the personalities changed and so did the issues. In a field of four candidates, two emerged as major contenders, sponsored by identifiable factions within the party. Conservatives, with great concern about the race issue, rallied behind I. Beverly Lake, a law professor from Wake Forest College. Moderates and liberals focused their hopes on a young, attractive, and dynamic candidate, Terry Sanford. Sanford had had very close connections

4. On North Carolina politics during the first half of this century see, V. O. Key, Jr., *Southern Politics* (New York: Random House, Inc., 1949), Chapter Ten, "North Carolina: Progressive Plutocracy."

with the Kerr Scott campaign and administration, which was relatively progressive by North Carolina standards. Sanford won, but not without a battle. Although he demonstrated considerable strength in the first primary, a runoff was requested. With the slate reduced to two candidates, Sanford polled a healthy margin, 56 per cent of the vote.

Throughout his administration Sanford led the state with a progressive and in some instances innovative program. By 1964 Sanford's faction felt enough strength and momentum to sponsor a candidate for the gubernatorial nomination. It selected Federal District Court Judge L. Richardson Preyer, who had been appointed to office by President Kennedy. The conservatives made a second bid for the nomination by supporting Lake. A third candidate emerged to capitalize on compromise. He staked his position in the middle and prided himself on coming from the Mountains. The candidate was Dan Moore, who hoped to moderate between the allegedly extreme positions of Preyer and Lake. The first primary indicated the party was split badly. Each of the major candidates won about a third of the vote, finishing in this order: Preyer (36.6 per cent), Moore (33.5 per cent), and Lake (28.2 per cent). The division had a very distinct geographical base illustrated in Figure VI. Immediately, the Lake and Moore factions combined their efforts, with Lake making a strong emotional appeal for Moore's candidacy. Governor Sanford appeared on statewide television to make public what everyone knew. He was strongly in favor of a Preyer victory. When the votes were counted in the second primary the success of the two strategies was clear. Moore won solidly by picking up virtually all the Lake vote, while Preyer's support was almost unchanged.

Over the last quarter century after the breakup of the "Shelby ring," politics in the Democratic party have not

Figure VI. DEMOCRATIC GUBERNATORIAL PRIMARY, MAY 30, 1964

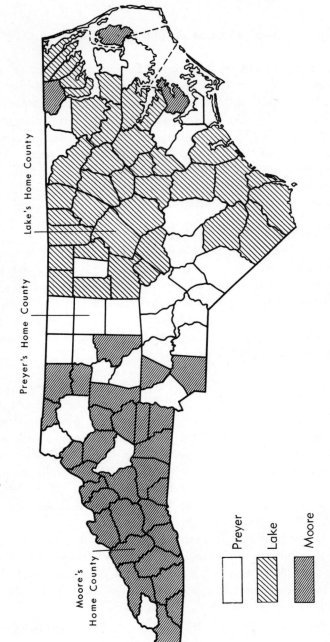

Lake's Home County

Preyer's Home County

Moore's
Home County

Preyer

Lake

Moore

Source: Based on data reported in the *North Carolina Manual,*
1965

been dominated by any single faction. Groups have appeared and disappeared depending on the political climate and personal ambitions. Coalitions, usually temporary, have formed and re-formed. Democrats have disagreed over who should be awarded the big prize—the governorship. But they have agreed that all factions must work together once that decision is made, because there is another party in the state. And they agree that that party should remain the minority.

Intraparty Competition: Republicans

The Republican party has used the convention to select its nominees for the various executive and legislative offices. Only occasionally has a primary been held. A look at the infrequent primaries does not tell much about the internal divisions of the party. However, some insight into the development of Republican party in the state is provided by such an examination.

Executive Offices. Since 1940 there have been eight primaries held by Republicans for five statewide executive offices. One primary each has been held for nomination to the offices of state treasurer, commissioner of agriculture, and governor. Primaries have been held twice for commissioner of insurance and three times for lieutenant governor. Three of the primaries were held before 1952, two in 1960, and three in 1964. Thus, the frequency of Republican primaries is on the rise.

In six primaries the number of contestants was limited to two; on two occasions the number was three. The winning candidates polled an average of 66 per cent of the vote, a respectable margin. No incumbents were involved, and no second primaries were necessary.

An examination of the number of voters participating

in Republican primaries indicates significant growth. While it must be remembered that the offices are not equal in appeal, comparison of votes is useful. In 1944 in a primary for state treasurer, the total vote was 6,725. In 1952 in electing a nominee for lieutenant governor 16,261 Republicans cast ballots. By 1960 a contest for the same office attracted 20,750 voters. And in 1964 the potential Republican nominees for lieutenant governor received a combined total of 54,783 votes. The 1964 Republican gubernatorial primary attracted the largest number of voters, 63,815. The figures attest to the fact that the reservoir of participants in the minority party's primary has grown dramatically and steadily in recent years.

The number of primary participants is quite small when compared to the number of Republican votes cast in the general election. However, the following figures do demonstrate growth:

	Primary Vote (A)	General Election Vote (B)	A as per cent of B
1952	16,261	374,530	4
1960	20,750	532,445	3
1964	54,783	526,727	10

The significant question is whether in future years even greater numbers will be attracted to the Republican Party and its primaries.

United States Congress: Senate. Only one primary has been held to select the Republican nominee for a position in the United States Senate. It took place in 1962, involved two candidates, and attracted 52,000 voters. The winning margin was 61 per cent. The number of votes cast in the primary was 16.1 per cent of the Republican vote cast in the general election of that year.

United States Congress: House of Representatives. During the period 1940-66 Republican primaries for congressional nominations have been held twelve times for regular terms and once for an unexpired term. Thus, less than 10 per cent of the nominations have been determined in primaries. Other devices—conventions or self-selection—have been used an extraordinarily large number of times.

Republican congressional primaries have not been held at any time during this period in five districts—First, Second, Third, Seventh and Eighth. All but the Eighth are districts in which there was a low level of competition for congressional nominations in the Democratic party and in which strong incumbents from that party served long terms in the national legislature. Thus, the presence of a strong incumbent from the Democratic party is probably related to absence of competition within both parties.

The other districts have been the sites of primary competition within the Republican party. The thirteen primaries have not been distributed equally among the districts. Three districts have had one primary each (Fourth, 1964; Fifth, 1962; and Eleventh, 1966); three districts have had two primaries (Sixth, 1950 and 1962; Ninth, 1944 and 1962; and Twelfth, 1958 and 1960);[5] and one district has had three (Tenth, 1948, 1964, and 1966). Also, the incidence of primaries has increased. Nine of the twelve contests occurred in the period 1958-66; only three before then. And the three were in 1950 or before. So it definitely appears that primary competition has been more frequent in recent years.

When contests did occur, they usually involved only two contestants, and the competition could be character-

5. The primary for unexpired term occurred in the Twelfth District along with a primary for a regular term.

ized as moderate to severe. One-third of the contests were settled by margins of less than 55 per cent; one-half of them by less than 61 per cent. None of the contests involved an incumbent Republican congressman and at no time was a second primary necessary.

These primaries have not attracted a great number of voters. The largest number participating was 14,292 in 1962 in the Ninth District. The median number of votes cast, however, is much less than half that figure (5,479)— also in 1962 in the Fifth District. This represents relatively few people compared with the number of Republican supporters in general elections. For example, in 1962 the votes cast in the Republican primaries in the Fifth and Ninth districts were 21 per cent and 17 per cent respectively of the votes cast for the Republican candidate in the November election.

Summary. The Republican party has not used the primary frequently to nominate its candidates for major political offices in the state. The few times that primary nominations have been made form a consistent pattern of political action. The contests usually involve two candidates and have never required a second primary. Competition, as measured by number of contests and margin of nominees' victory, is greater for congressional nominations than for state executive positions.

Possibly more important is the fact that more people are participating in recent statewide Republican primaries. The number is still small compared with the number of Republican votes cast in the general election, but the former as a percentage of the latter has increased over the period. Finally, the frequency of Republican primaries has increased. Three-fourths of the primary contests in the minority party since 1940 have occurred in the last eight years (1958-1966).

Conventions and other party devices are used to determine most nominees. Without access to those deliberations, further examination of the internal politics of the Republican party is impossible.

CHAPTER FIVE ⊠

INTERPARTY COMPETITION

In the period 1940-66 competition between the two major political parties in North Carolina has been changing. Gradually and irregularly competition between the Democrats and the Republicans has grown stronger. This developing competition is not based upon the parties alternating in control of office. The Democrats have to this point maintained their majority party status in most contests. What does characterize the competition is the decreasing strength of the Democrats and the increasing and intensifying challenge of the traditional minority, the Republicans. However, while politics is becoming competitive, that stage has not been reached at all levels and for all offices.

This structure of competition is not new to North Carolina. In fact, Republicans and Democrats were very strong competitors during the period after the Civil War. In presidential elections the competition was closest and continued, with few exceptions, until 1904. During this period (1868-1900) North Carolina cast a majority vote for two Republican Presidents, and the Democratic candidate never won by margins of more than 54 per cent. In 1928 the Republican candidate for President, Herbert Hoover, won a comfortable but still competitive majority as the state Democratic party was split over Al Smith. During the Roosevelt era (1932-44) Democratic margins of victory averaged 70 per cent.

Interparty competition since the Civil War has been less severe in contests for the state's chief executive post, although gubernatorial races were relatively close from 1868 through 1896. During the period of "recovery politics," the Republicans won the governorship three times, and they frequently managed to draw 45 to 49 per cent of the vote when losing; but from 1900 up to the period of focus in this study, the Democrats held a stronger majority in gubernatorial contests than in presidential politics. The high point of this strong majority (1940) opens the last quarter-century of North Carolina politics.

We have characterized the period 1940-66 as one of significant change in the relative strength of the state's two major political parties. However, it is important to point out that a different pattern of interparty competition exists for the several types of officials elected. Figure VII graphically portrays the differences for President, governor, and the congressional delegation.

Executive Offices: National and State

The most competitive politics has been in the state's vote for President. No Republican presidential candidate

Table 12   North Carolina Presidential Votes, 1940-64

Year	Democrat	Republican	Other
1940	74.0%	26.0%	–
1944	66.7	33.3	–
1948	58.0	32.7	9.3%
1952	53.9	46.1	–
1956	50.7	49.3	–
1960	52.1	47.9	–
1964	56.2	43.8	–

Sources: Based on data reported in the appropriate volumes of the *North Carolina Manual*; and in Donald R. Matthews, *et al.* (compilers), *North Carolina Votes* (Chapel Hill: The University of North Carolina Press, 1962).

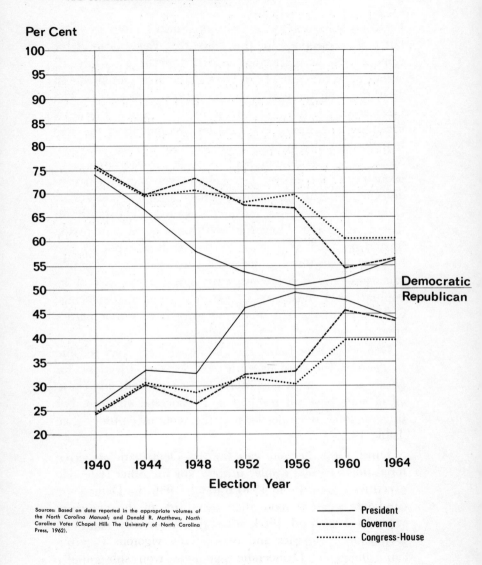

Figure VII. DEMOCRATIC AND REPUBLICAN VOTES IN PRESIDENTIAL, GUBERNATORIAL, AND CONGRESSIONAL ELECTIONS, 1940-64

Per Cent

Democratic
Republican

Election Year

Sources: Based on data reported in the appropriate volumes of the *North Carolina Manual;* and Donald R. Matthews, *North Carolina Votes* (Chapel Hill: The University of North Carolina Press, 1962).

——————— President
----------- Governor
················· Congress-House

has been able to get a majority of North Carolina's votes, but it is in elections for this office that Republicans have come closest to statewide victory. Indeed, as Table 12 shows, from the peak of the Democratic presidential vote in 1940 the direction was down dramatically until 1960. The Democratic margin was lowest in 1956 when President Eisenhower, running as a popular incumbent, came close to making history in the state by winning its electoral votes. Since 1952 presidential politics in North Carolina have been quite competitive. The Eisenhower and Nixon candidacies and the increasingly pro-civil rights position of Democratic candidates have contributed significantly to that development. However, in this period of nationwide flux in presidential politics North Carolina is one of two southern states that has not voted a majority for a Republican candidate. It has consistently given a majority of its popular votes and all of its electoral votes to Democrats. Only once in the last quarter-century have minor parties appeared on North Carolina ballots.

Democrats have found the Old North State very reliable in contests for state executive offices also. Elections for governor, lieutenant governor, attorney general, and council of state have all resulted in Democratic victories; but these victories have not been of the same magnitude. (See Table 13.)

Until 1960 the vote cast for the Democratic gubernatorial nominee was similar to those for the other statewide executive offices. From 1940 through 1956 the Democratic candidate received more than two-thirds of the two-party vote. In 1960 and 1964, after two vigorously contested Democratic primaries and two equally vigorous Republican campaigns, Democratic nominees won substantially fewer votes. In 1960 and 1964 the Republicans could

Table 13   General Election Competition for State Executive Offices, 1940-64

Office	Number of elections[1]	Number uncontested	Number with incumbents	Average Democratic vote in contested elections	Average Democratic vote—all elections	Average Republican vote—all elections	Number won by 60 per cent or more
Governor	7	0	1	—	66.3	33.7	5
Lieutenant Governor	7	0	0	—	67.3	32.7	6
Attorney General	7	0	7	—	67.7	32.3	7
Secretary of State	7	0	7	—	67.8	32.2	7
Auditor	8	1	8	67.7	71.7	28.3	8
Treasurer	8	0	7	—	67.6	32.4	8
Superintendent of Public Instruction	8	2	8	68.8	76.6	23.4	8
Commissioner of Agriculture	8	1	7	67.7	71.8	28.2	8
Commissioner of Insurance	9	0	9	—	66.8	33.2	8
Commissioner of Labor	8	2	8	68.8	76.6	23.4	8

1. There were seven regular-term elections. Number varies because of special elections.
Sources: Based on data reported in the appropriate volumes of the *North Carolina Manual*.

claim some progress in their bids for the governorship, as is indicated in the following figures:

Democrat			Republican		
1960	Sanford	735,248 (54%)	Gavin	613,975 (46%)
1964	Moore	790,343 (57%)	Gavin	606,165 (43%)

In 1960 Robert Gavin, the Republican nominee, received 45.5 per cent of the votes. The Democrats were reminded that the last time their candidate received less than 55 per cent of the vote was in 1896, when a Republican, Daniel Russell was elected. In 1964 Gavin was renominated. The Republicans did not do as well, but they did approximate a competitive position. In both cases the Republican successes in attracting a larger number of votes followed very intensely fought Democratic nominating primaries. Undoubtedly, the two are related. Many Republicans, pondering the results, were aware that more effort, more time, and different candidates might improve their position, and Democrats were increasingly convinced that politics had changed. After the 1966 congressional elections leaders of both parties were publicly and seriously discussing the chances for Republican victory in 1968. But one fact remains. North Carolina is the only former Confederate state that in this period has not voted a majority for either a Republican presidential or gubernatorial candidate.

Results of elections for lieutenant governor, attorney general, and council of state indicate that these nine offices have very similar structures of competition. Votes cast for these several offices are quite consistent from one position to another as shown in Table 13. No office is substantially more or less competitive than the others. Except when a candidate ran unopposed, as occurred six times during the period, the Democratic majorities are amazingly similar.

Even though some offices have had the same Democratic nominee throughout much of the period, the pattern has not been disturbed. For example, the Democratic nominee for secretary of state throughout this period has been Thad Eure. Despite his repeated and regular appearance on the ticket his portions of the two-party vote are not very different from those of the five different Democratic nominees for commissioner of insurance. Individual nominees cannot gain much attention when voters cast straight-ticket ballots for these state executives.

Two additional factors that have potential impact on the structure of competition deserve mention. Republicans consistently opposed the Democratic nominees even though their chances of success were remote. In only six of the seventy elections was the Democrat running without competition. In all but nine contests the Democratic candidate was an incumbent who had the advantages of office and experience.

A final pattern is the decreasing majorities that the winning candidates receive. In 1940 the average for the nine offices was 76 per cent; in 1948, 72 per cent; in 1956, 67 per cent; and in 1964, 62 per cent. While the pattern of support is not regular, its over-all direction is consistent. However, it is important to recognize that the Democratic nominees for these executive positions continue to receive substantial majorities. Such elections cannot be considered competitive.

Competition for President and governor has spread gradually through the state since 1940. However, the development of competition has not been identical for the two executive offices even though the direction of the competition has been similar. Competition in presidential and gubernatorial elections has differed both in intensity and pace. Table 14 provides supporting data.

Table 14 Number of Counties with Various Levels of Democratic Votes, 1940-64

Office	Date	Per Cent Votes for Democratic Candidate					
		70+	60-70	55-60	50-55	45-50	45-below
President	1940	62	20	6	5	4	3
	1944	49	20	10	5	7	9
	1948	35	18	8	9	15	15
	1952	29	18	4	17	13	19
	1956	28	14	5	10	19	24
	1960	30	12	10	9	14	25
	1964	13	34	34	16	6	7
Governor	1940	66	16	7	6	2	3
	1944	58	13	8	9	4	8
	1948	64	12	11	7	3	3
	1952	53	13	12	10	6	6
	1956	53	13	12	9	8	5
	1960	34	14	6	19	13	4
	1964	34	19	14	14	10	9

Sources: Based on data reported in the appropriate volumes of the *North Carolina Manual*; and in Donald R. Matthews, *et al.* (compilers), *North Carolina Votes.*

In 1940 approximately two-thirds of the state's one hundred counties gave the Democratic candidates for these two offices at least 70 per cent of their votes. Another one-fourth supported the Democratic party with majorities between 55 and 70 per cent. Very few counties voted Republican majorities. Indeed, less than one-tenth of the counties could be considered competitive in that the winning party received margins of 5 per cent or less.

Significant change was manifest in presidential contests by 1952. In that year less than half of the counties were overwhelmingly Democratic (60 per cent or more) and approximately one-third of the counties voted a Republican majority. By 1960 the number of dominant Democratic counties was forty-two, whereas the Republican candidate won in thirty-nine counties.

In the most recent presidential contest the "southern strategy" of the Republican candidate cut into the Democrats' stronghold in the east, significantly reducing the number of counties voting 70 per cent or more for the Democratic candidate. Whether this was a temporary flirtation of defecting Democrats or a more fundamental change of affiliation based on the civil rights policies of the Democratic administration must await future contests. Goldwater's candidacy also decreased by two-thirds the number of counties that went for the Republican nominee.

In gubernatorial politics, competition came with more deliberate speed. In 1952 two-thirds of the counties gave the Democratic candidate at least 60 per cent of their votes and most majorities exceeded 70 per cent. Meanwhile, only twelve counties went Republican. By 1960 less than half of the counties were overwhelmingly Democratic, and the number of Republican majorities inched up. Politics for the state's highest executive post has intensified considerably since 1960. The number of counties with Republican majorities has increased fourfold. The number of counties giving Democrats as least 60 per cent of the vote has been reduced by almost half.

Throughout the period the heavily Democratic counties have been located principally in the east. The base of Republicanism in 1940 was the Mountain counties with a tradition based on the Civil War and the party of the Union. Competition since 1940 has grown from this area, through the industrialized and urbanized Piedmont, and gradually into the eastern Democratic stronghold.

Significant areas of growth for the Republican party are the metropolitan counties in the state.[1] If the vote of

1. Urban Republicanism has been the subject of recent research. See D. Strong, *Urban Republicanism in the South* (University, Alabama: University of Alabama Press, 1960), and B. Cosman, "Presi-

six counties with the largest urban area is examined, the growth of competition is manifest. The Republican party is receiving significantly more votes today in these areas than at the beginning of the period. Table 15 provides data on which this conclusion is based. It also indicates a difference between presidential and gubernatorial electorates.

Table 15   Republican Vote by Sectors, 1940-64

Office	Year	Metropolitan Per cent Republican	Non metropolitan per cent Republican	Percentage point difference, metropolitan and nonmetropolitan	State per cent Republican
President	1940	22.1	27.1	−5.0	26.0
	1944	29.7	34.3	−4.6	33.3
	1948	38.6	35.1	3.5	32.7
	1952	50.6	44.6	6.0	46.1
	1956	56.8	47.2	9.6	49.3
	1960	53.1	46.2	6.9	47.9
	1964	45.1	43.5	2.4	43.8
Governor	1940	18.5	25.9	−7.4	24.3
	1944	22.9	32.5	−9.6	30.4
	1948	21.9	27.8	−5.9	26.4
	1952	30.7	32.2	−1.5	32.5
	1956	33.6	32.9	.7	33.0
	1960	51.1	43.7	7.4	45.5
	1964	47.3	42.1	5.2	43.4

Sources: Based on data reported in the appropriate volumes of the *North Carolina Manual*; and in Donald R. Matthews, *et al.* (compilers), *North Carolina Votes*.

dential Republicanism in the South, 1960," *Journal of Politics* 24 (May, 1966), 303-22. The problem of maintaining urban strength is examined in B. Cosman, *Five States for Goldwater* (University, Alabama: University of Alabama Press, 1967). This section was assisted greatly by ideas expressed in these writings.

In recent elections—with the exception of 1964—a majority of the metropolitan votes in North Carolina has gone to the Republican presidential candidate. This pattern first appeared in 1952. From 1940 to 1952 the Republican vote gain in presidential elections in urban areas was 28.5 percentage points. During the same period the Republican gain in nonmetropolitan counties was 17.5 points and the statewide vote 20.1 points. A similar, although not so striking, pattern occurred in gubernatorial elections. The metropolitan vote gain was 12.2 points, the nonmetropolitan gain was 6.3 points, and the statewide vote gain was 8.2 points. Since 1948 in presidential elections and since 1956 in gubernatorial elections, the Republican vote in the metropolitan counties has exceeded the Republican strength in the statewide totals.

The fact that an important source of Republican votes has developed in metropolitan areas should not overshadow the Republican increases in nonmetropolitan North Carolina. Republican growth in the latter areas has been less dramatic but not less significant. It does show that political competition for these two major offices is not restricted to a specific kind of population or area in the state.

This fact about North Carolina politics was made quite clear in the 1964 election when Republicans received larger numbers of votes in the solid Democratic counties of the east (see Figures VIII and IX). Within that area the Republican presidential candidate received more votes than any previous GOP hopeful. This phenomenon of Republicanism invading traditional Democratic counties was shared by many other southern counties with large Negro populations. In fact, in 1964 Republicans gained more over the 1960 campaign in these counties of North Carolina than in any other section of the state. These gains almost offset the losses that were suffered by the Republi-

Figure VIII. PRESIDENTIAL ELECTION, 1964

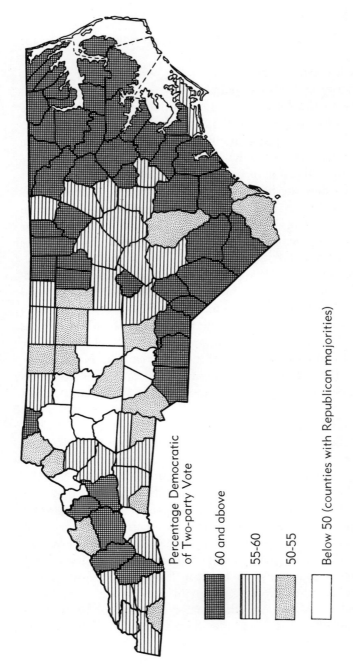

Percentage Democratic
of Two-party Vote

60 and above

55-60

50-55

Below 50 (counties with Republican majorities)

Source: Based on data reported in the *North Carolina Manual,* 1967

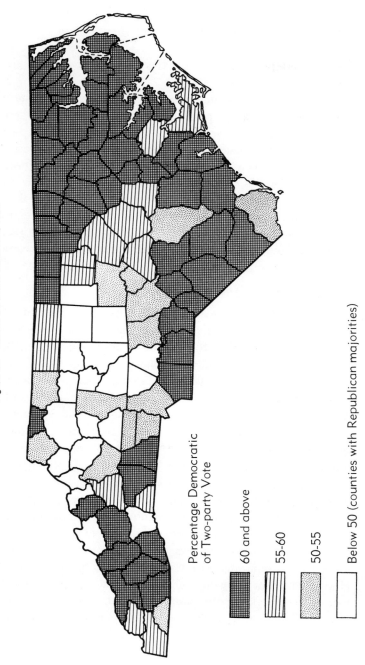

Figure IX. GUBERNATORIAL ELECTION, 1964

Percentage Democratic
of Two-party Vote

60 and above

55-60

50-55

Below 50 (counties with Republican majorities)

Source: Based on data reported in the *North Carolina Manual*
1967

can candidate in traditionally Republican counties of the west.

While Democratic margins were lower in the eastern half of the state, it is possible that the Negroes in these very same counties, in many cases voting for the first time, kept the counties strongly in the Democratic column. In reviewing the 1964 election, the Southern Regional Council said that there is a strong possibility that North Carolina would have gone Republican if it had not been for the Negro vote. And the Negro votes in eastern counties and in other areas of the state were cast for the Democratic candidate. These votes helped maintain the Democratic party as the majority party.

Legislative: United States Congress

In national and state legislative politics, the changes in relative strength of the two major parties are consistent with those developing for executive positions. However, they are revealed in a different manner and have achieved a different magnitude. Unlike executive elections, legislative elections have been won by Republicans. Tables 16 and 17 summarize competition in congressional elections.

North Carolina's two seats in the United States Senate have been held by Democrats who have received wide margins of support throughout the period. At the beginning and end of the period strong Democratic incumbents dominated the senatorial scene. Twice during the period (both in 1954) Democratic nominees were unopposed. On four occasions the contest did not involve an incumbent because of fights within the Democratic party. Until 1960 Democratic majorities averaged two-thirds or more of the vote. But competition has changed, the margins of victory for the majority party have declined. Incumbent Senator B. Everett Jordan received 61 per cent of the vote

Table 16 General Election Competition for Congressional Offices, 1940-66

Office	Number of elections	Number uncontested	Number with incumbents	Average Democratic vote in contested elections	Average Democratic vote—all elections	Average Republican vote—all elections	Number won by 60 per cent or more
U.S. Senate							
Position 1	5	1	5	66.5	73.3	26.7	5
Position 2	8	1	4	65.2	69.6	30.4	7
U.S. House District							
1st	15	3	14	81.4	85.1	14.9	15
2nd	14	9	13	87.9	95.7	4.3	14
3rd	14	4	13	76.5	81.6	18.4	14
4th	14	2	14	67.2	71.9	28.1	11
5th	14	1	10	65.7	68.2	31.8	8
6th	14	2	13	67.8	72.4	27.6	11
7th	14	3	12	82.9	86.6	13.4	14
8th	14	0	10	58.3	58.3	41.7	4
9th	14	1	13	54.7	57.9	42.1	5
10th	14	0	9	52.7	52.7	47.3	3
11th	14	3	10	62.4	70.5	29.5	11
12th	10	0	5	60.4	60.4	39.6	7

Sources: Based on data reported in the appropriate volume of the *North Carolina Manual*.

Table 17   Party Strength in State's Congressional Delegation, 1941-67

Year	Senate		House[1]	
	Democrat	Republican	Democrat	Republican
1941	2	0	11	0
1943	2	0	12	0
1945	2	0	12	0
1947	2	0	12	0
1949	2	0	12	0
1951	2	0	12	0
1953·	2	0	11	1
1955	2	0	11	1
1957	2	0	11	1
1959	2	0	11	1
1961	2	0	11	1
1963	2	0	9	2
1965	2	0	?	2
1967	2	0	8	3

1. In 1940 North Carolina had eleven seats in the House of Representatives. This was increased to twelve from 1942 to 1961. The 1961 reapportionment resulted in a loss of one seat. Currently, North Carolina has eleven seats in the House.

Sources: Based on data reported in the appropriate volumes of the *North Carolina Manual.*

in 1960 and 55.5 pr cent in 1966. In 1964 Senator Sam J. Ervin, Jr., received 60 per cent of the vote. Republicans did not focus on these elections until in 1966 when their candidate John Shallcross traveled throughout the state, appealing for votes. Despite its lack of attention to senatorial politics the minority party has improved its position.

In elections for the state's delegation to the United States House of Representatives, two-party competition has increased but not on a statewide basis. Republicans have gained a slow, small, but steady foothold in congressional politics. However, the Democrats have maintained their position as a strong majority in most districts.

In 54 per cent of the elections since 1940, **Democratic**

congressional candidates polled more than two-thirds of the votes; in seven of ten elections the Democratic margin was at least 60 per cent. But these figures do not distinguish between districts. Table 16 provides details on the districts. If three measures of competition are used—average Democratic percentage, number of contests unopposed, and percent of elections won by 60 per cent or more of the vote—three categories of districts emerge. In the first category are the Second, Seventh, First, and Third Districts. In the four districts the average Democratic vote has been above 80 per cent, with Democrats always winning by more than 60 per cent. These high percentages can be attributed partially to the fact that in approximately one-third of the elections the Democrat was unopposed. The extreme case in this group is the Second District where nine elections have been uncontested and Democrats have won by an average of 95.7 per cent. Although the precise composition of these districts has changed since 1940, they include all eastern counties from the Virginia border to the South Carolina border. Republicans did not receive much encouragement in any of these districts until recently. In 1966, however, Republicans made a determined effort in the First District by running a conservative college professor against a recently elected conservative Democrat. Although the 40 per cent barrier was not broken by the minority, it claimed a victory in reducing the winning margin from 83 per cent in 1964 to 61 per cent in 1966, an impressive change.

The second group of districts includes the Sixth, Fourth, Eleventh, and Fifth. These districts have more similarities than those in the first group. The average Democratic vote was 71 per cent. A total of eight elections held during this period have been uncontested. Only once in these four districts has a Republican won the elections, that being in the Fourth District in 1966. Three districts in this group are composed of upper Piedmont counties. The Eleventh District from 1941 to 1961 was composed of seven southwestern Mountain counties. Since 1961 it has contained all southwestern Mountain counties.

The last four districts (Eighth, Ninth, Tenth, and Twelfth) are approaching two-party competition, but still have a way to go. They are most competitive in the sense that virtually all elections are contested. Nearly two-thirds of the elections have been decided by margins of less than 60 per cent. The average Democratic percentage has been 57. Most of the Republican congressional victories in the state have been in the Eighth, Ninth, and Tenth districts. The four districts are located in lower and western Piedmont and Mountain areas. From 1941 to 1961 the Twelfth District was located in the far southwestern corner of the state.

With some variations the pattern of congressional politics is one of increasing competition from the Coastal Plain, through the upper Piedmont, and to the lower Piedmont and Mountains. The least competition is in the east, and competition increases as one moves west. However, until recently these politics over the period have generally not been very competitive.

As in contests for other offices, however, patterns are changing in congressional politics. The solid Democratic hold on the state's public offices was broken in 1952 when Republican Charles R. Jonas was elected from the Tenth congressional district. Jonas was the first Republican congressman from North Carolina since his father was elected in 1928. In defeating the incumbent Democratic congressman, Hamilton C. Jones, Jonas carried every county in the district. The interest in the contest is revealed by the fact that the electorate more than doubled from the previous one (64,182 in 1950; 143,577 in 1952). Jonas continued to amass large majorities in his bids for re-election. With the exception of the 1958 election, Jonas regularly received more than 57 per cent of the votes until 1962. In 1962 Jonas found himself in a different district, that one observer writes was drawn to eliminate the lone minority party congressman.[2] Jonas once again defeated the incumbent Democratic congressman.

Rather than reducing the number of Republican congressmen from North Carolina, the 1962 elections saw the Republican delegation increased. James Broyhill joined Jonas as the second Republican member of the delegation. Broyhill also defeated an incumbent Democrat, Hugh Q. Alexander, to serve as the representative of the Ninth congressional district. Jonas' strength was based in Mecklenburg County, site of the largest city in the state. Broyhill's strength rests in maintaining Republican counties that often supported Republican presidential and gubernatorial candidates. Broyhill has also won increasing favor with his constituents. In 1964 he received 55 per cent of the vote. In 1966, despite a vigorous challenge from his Democratic opponent who had campaign assistance from high-level state officials, Broyhill amassed a plurality of 34,000 in receiving 63 per cent of the votes.

The year 1966 was good for the Republicans in other areas of the state. The most significant event was the victory of a third Republican congressman, James Gardner, over Harold Cooley, the dean of the state's congressional delegation. Cooley had served in Congress since 1934. Furthermore, Cooley had been the chairman of the House Agricultural Committee since 1949, with the exception of

2. See Virgil C. Stroud, "A Political Maneuver That Backfired," *Western Political Quarterly,* XVII (1964), 125-33.

the Eighty-Third Congress, when he was ranking minority member. A third significant fact about the victory was that Gardner received major support from Wake County, where a significant segment of the population is employed by the state, many of them receiving their jobs through the Democratic party. Finally, the presence of Gardner among successful Republicans increased the resources available to the minority party to strengthen its position in state politics.

There are several common features of the three congressional victories for the Republican party since 1952. In all cases the Republican candidate defeated an incumbent congressman. This alone is a major accomplishment in any congressional district by any minority candidate.[3] In the cases of the two Republicans who to date have run for re-election, they have been able to enlarge their electoral bases. Only in 1958 did Jonas have genuinely close competition from his Democratic opponent. Broyhill has increased his pluralities steadily and significantly in his two bids for re-election. Whether this pattern will continue is yet to be seen. It would appear that the Republican congressmen could become almost as safe in their districts as the Democrats in theirs unless, of course, those districts are restructured to their disadvantage.

We have focused at some length on the three cases of success for the state's Republican party in winning congressional elections because they represent the highest

3. Recent figures indicate that nationwide over the past decade only around 6 per cent of the incumbents running for re-election are defeated. The number of incumbents defeated in the South is almost infinitesimal. See C. O. Jones, "The Role of the Campaign in Congressional Politics," *in* M. K. Jennings and L. H. Zeigler (eds.), *The Electoral Process* (Englewood Cliffs, N.J.: Prentice-Hall, Inc., 1966), p. 24.

offices won by that party in North Carolina since 1940. This should now be supplemented by looking at the state-wide picture of competition for congressional offices. Only in this way can a proper perspective on the structure of competition at this level be achieved. A comprehensive set of data is given in Table 18. The general picture of inter-

Table 18   Two-Party Competition for Congressional Offices, 1940-66

	Per Cent of Congressional Elections won by Designated Margins			
	50-54.9	55-59.9	60-99.9	Unopposed
1940-58	5 (3)	13 (8)	70 (42)	12 (7)
1950-58	10 (6)	13 (8)	53 (32)	24 (14)
1960-66	17 (8)	31 (14)	37 (17)	15 (7)

Sources: Based on data reported in the appropriate volumes of the *North Carolina Manual.*

party competition for congressional offices is one of slow, steady, but continually increasing competition. Figures in Table 18, which give the percentage of congressional elections that were decided by three levels of competition or were unopposed, supports this conclusion. There are still some Democratic candidates who run unopposed. In fact, in this particular category the progress of the minority party is statistically nil. But when there are candidates from the two major parties for the congressional seats, the competition grows keener. The number of contests won by 60 per cent or more of the votes has been decreased from almost three-fourths (70 per cent) to just over one-third (37 per cent). The number of those that are decided by less than 5 percentage points has more than tripled. This was highlighted in 1966 when Republican candidates polled more votes than Democratic candidates in those districts where both parties had nominees.

Legislative: General Assembly

As is mentioned in the Introduction, state legislative politics has recently undergone a change resulting from the United States Supreme Court enunciation of the "one-man-one-vote" principle in 1963 and the subsequent application of that principle to state legislative districting in 1964. Until the reapportionment and redistricting of the North Carolina House of Representatives in 1965, each county in the state had at least one member in that body and the larger counties were given additional representation based on population. State Senate districts were apportioned according to population. In 1965 both houses of the General Assembly were apportioned on a population basis and legislative districts were redrawn.

The examination of electoral competition for the two houses of the General Assembly is based on elections held in 1952 and subsequent years. Competition will be measured by three standards: the number of contested seats, the frequency of party success, and the level of electoral support. In addition, the analysis will briefly focus on location and sources of support for the two parties.[4]

The number of legislative seats that have been uncontested by the Republican party has varied since 1952, but in a number of districts Democrats win by default because they have no opposition. In the past fifteen years the portion of uncontested elections, as shown in Table 19, has

4. In this analysis I have had access to a recently published study by Malcolm E. Jewell, *Legislative Representation in the Contemporary South* (Durham, N.C.: Duke University Press, 1967), Chapter Four. I am grateful to Professor Jewell for his cooperation in sharing his findings with me before they were published. I have depended greatly on them.

Table 19 Two-Party Competition in State Legislative Elections,
1952-66

Year	Per cent of Legislative Seats Uncontested by Republicans	
	Senate	House
1952	54	47
1954	50	47
1956	68	67
1958	58	51
1960	56	51
1962	42	39
1964	42	33
1966	48	50

Source: Adapted from M. Jewell, *Legislative Representation in the Contemporary South* (Durham, N.C.: Duke University Press, 1967), Chapter Four.

ranged from 42 per cent to 68 per cent in the Senate and from 39 per cent to 67 per cent in the House. The pattern within each house is erratic, except that since 1960 competition has been slightly greater than before. Contests are more frequent in the House than in the Senate. This may be due to the fact that until reapportionment the basic pattern of House representation was protected by the constitutional requirement that each county be given a minimum of one member. Thus, these districts were not subject to gerrymandering or other forms of political maneuvering.

The success of the parties in winning legislative elections has also been erratic. Table 20 gives the proportion of legislative seats won by each party since 1940. Until 1966 Republicans were barely noticed in the state Senate. They always had at least one member of the fifty-member body, but never more than three. In 1966 they doubled their previous record by winning seven Senate seats. Republican success in the state House has been greater. They have had as few as four members but as many as twenty-

Table 20   Party Strength in the General Assembly of North Carolina, 1941-67

Year	Senate		House	
	Democrat	Republican	Democrat	Republican
1941	48	2	114	6
1943	48	2	108	12
1945	47	3	106	14
1947	48	2	108	12
1949	48	2	109	11
1951	48	2	110	10
1953	48	2	106	14
1955	49	1	110	10
1957	47	3	107	13
1959	49	1	116	4
1961	48	2	105	15
1963	48	2	99	21
1965	49	1	106	14
1967	43	7	94	26

Sources: Based on data reported in the appropriate volumes of the *North Carolina Manual*.

six; this number was elected in 1966 and was the largest state legislative electoral delegation for the Republicans since 1929 when they had thirty-six in the House and thirteen in the Senate. The significance of this high mark is only partially seen in the number of seats held. In 1966 Republicans contested half the legislative seats in the two houses. They won almost half of the House contests in which they were engaged and slightly less than one-third of the Senate contests. Of course, the fact that they did not field more candidates in the legislative elections may indicate that they could not reasonably compete in them.

Democratic and Republican support is not spread evenly throughout the state. The level and location of electoral support for the two parties is indicated in Figures X-XIII. The maps are based on legislative elections in selected years since 1952. Four elections were held before the 1965

Figure X. PARTY COMPETITION FOR THE GENERAL ASSEMBLY: Senate, 1952, 1956, 1958, 1960

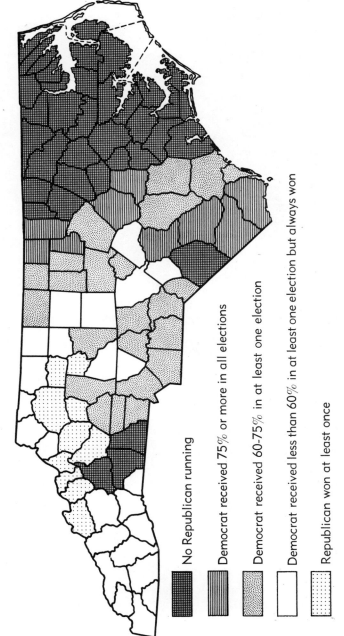

No Republican running

Democrat received 75% or more in all elections

Democrat received 60-75% in at least one election

Democrat received less than 60% in at least one election but always won

Republican won at least once

Source: Based on data reported in John L. Sanders, *Data on North Carolina Congressional Districts, State Senatorial Districts, and Apportionment of the State House of Representatives* (Chapel Hill: Institute of Government, 1961).

Figure XI. PARTY COMPETITION FOR THE GENERAL ASSEMBLY: House, 1952, 1956, 1958, 1960

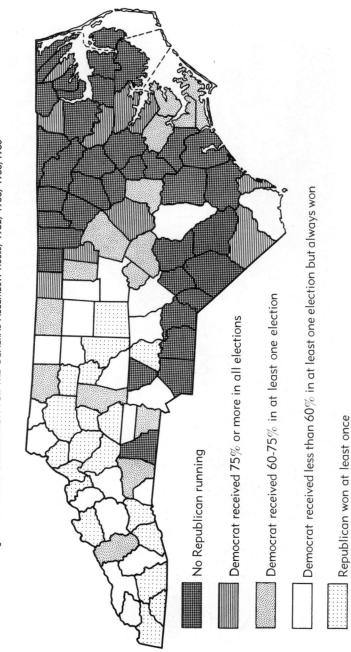

No Republican running

Democrat received 75% or more in all elections

Democrat received 60-75% in at least one election

Democrat received less than 60% in at least one election but always won

Republican won at least once

Source: Based on data reported in John L. Sanders, *Data on North Carolina Congressional Districts, State Senatorial Districts, and Apportionment of the State House of Representatives* (Chapel Hill: Institute of Government, 1961).

Figure XII. PARTY COMPETITION FOR THE GENERAL ASSEMBLY: Senate, 1966

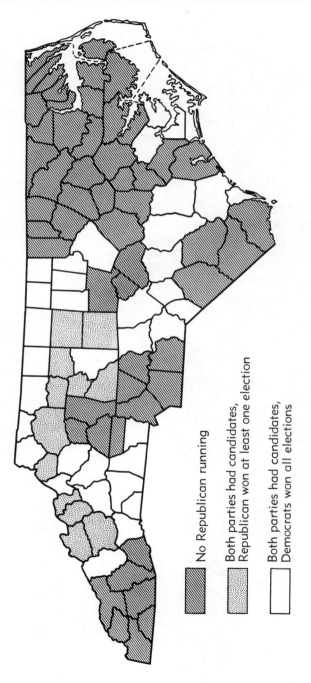

No Republican running

Both parties had candidates,
Republican won at least one election

Both parties had candidates,
Democrats won all elections

Source: Based on data reported in State Board of Elections,
North Carolina Legislative Elections, 1966.

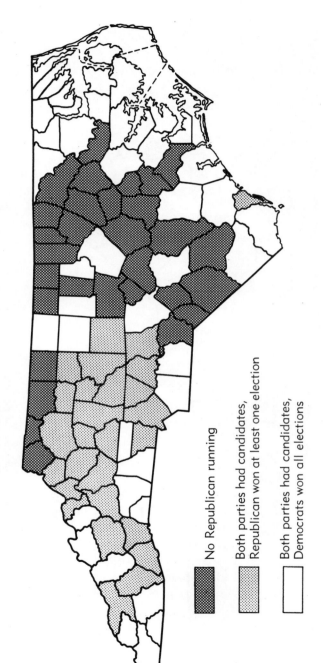

Figure XIII. PARTY COMPETITION FOR THE GENERAL ASSEMBLY: House, 1966

No Republican running

Both parties had candidates, Republican won at least one election

Both parties had candidates, Democrats won all elections

Source: Based on data reported in State Board of Elections, *North Carolina Legislative Elections, 1966.*

reapportionment and redistricting. Results of these elections are presented in Figures X and XI. Election results for the 1966 elections are reported in Figures XII and XIII.

In the four House elections before 1965 there were thirty-six counties in which Democratic candidates won without Republican opposition. There were another twenty counties in which Democratic candidates, when opposed, received at least 60 per cent of the vote. During this period at least two-thirds of the Democrats won by margins of 60 per cent or more. Most of the counties are located in the eastern half of the state. Seventeen counties have had at least one Republican representative during the period. Those with the most consistent Republican majorities are Alexander, Avery, Davie, Mitchell, Watauga, Wilkes, and Yadkin. Most are in the upper Mountains section. After the 1966 reapportionment and redistricting, electoral competition for the state House changed significantly. Twelve districts had uncontested elections. One of these was won by a Republican. Thus, more than three-fourths of the districts had contests, although there were not always full slates from the minority party. Republicans won at least one seat in each of seventeen districts. Major examples of incomplete Republican slates include districts containing the state's largest urban areas: Asheville, Charlotte, Durham, Greensboro, Raleigh, and Winston-Salem. In these districts Republicans had candidates for fourteen of the twenty-nine seats, with major deficiencies in Guilford (Greensboro) and Mecklenburg (Charlotte) counties.

In the North Carolina Senate elections before 1965 approximately one-third of the districts were won by the Democrats without opposition or with more than 75 per cent of the vote. Another one-fourth of the districts had a Democratic margin of no less than 60 per cent. In each of the four elections at least thirty-two Democratic senators won by a majority of 60 per cent or more. Three districts had at least one Republican senator during the period.

Senate districts were different in 1966 and so was electoral competition for Senate membership. The map in Figure XII shows contradiction in the change. More districts (almost half) were won by Democrats without opposition and more districts elected at least one Republican senator. Republican difficulties in recruiting candidates spread to the southeast, lower Piedmont, and southwest. Democrats continued to face difficulty in the Mountains and experienced new difficulties in the Piedmont.

Malcolm Jewell suggests that legislative competition and success for the Republican party is most likely to come from three sources: traditionally Republican counties, metropolitan counties, and counties which have recently supported Republican presidential candidates.[5] In North Carolina a slight majority of the candidates and an overwhelming number of the Republican legislators come from those counties, principally in the mountains, where Republicanism can be traced to the Civil War and Reconstruction. The second highest number of minority party candidates and legislators come from counties which have given Republican presidential candidates a high proportion of the votes in recent years.

The metropolitan counties, though the source of much recent southern Republicanism, have not provided as many Republican legislative candidates and legislators as might be expected. In these metropolitan areas, which are frequently better organized and which probably have a larger pool of potential candidates, the North Carolina Republi-

5. *Idem.*

can party has had problems in recruiting. In 1966 a full slate was impossible in Forsyth, Guilford, and Mecklenbury counties.

Recent Republican success in state legislative elections have had significant impact on the organization and operation of the North Carolina General Assembly. In 1967 the Democrats for the first time in recent history had a majority party organization with formally elected party leaders and occasional caucuses to determine party strategy. This organization took place after the Republicans elected their leadership and demonstrated their willingness to be an organized opposition by presenting candidates for speaker of the house and president pro tempore of the Senate and introducing a number of proposals for consideration by the General Assembly.

SUMMARY AND CONCLUSIONS

The survey of the nature of competition within and between the two major parties of the state highlights aspects of the changing political scene in North Carolina. Two general dimensions of intra- and interparty competition in North Carolina over the last twenty-five years appear. Democratic party politics has not been dominated by a single, durable, rigid faction. No group has had firm control of this major party. And the Democrats' hold on the reins of political power in the state has become less firm as Republican support has increased gradually at all levels and for most offices.

Democratic factionalism has not involved fragmentation. But, just as important, it has not been controlled by any particular group. The various state administrations have not been successful in extending their power by determining their successors. The Gardner faction was unable to maintain its hold in 1940 and 1948. And the Kerr Scott, Hodges, and Sanford factions could not project their influence on the electorate in successive elections. Controlling groups in Democratic statewide politics have changed frequently.

Competition between Republicans and Democrats has grown sharper. The largest Republican majorities in statewide contests have been achieved in the presidential elections and more recently in gubernatorial contests. Impressive victories have been gained by the Republicans in congressional politics and Republican candidates have nibbled away at Democratic majorities in many other districts. Even in contests for council of state, United

States senator, and state legislative seats, Republicans have increased their voting strength. But despite the changes, Democrats still hold these posts with substantial majorities.

What do the increased competition resulting in changing factional control within the Democratic party and an occasional victory for the Republican party mean for state politics? What are some of the problems and prospects for the Republican and Democratic parties in North Carolina? First, a look at the minority party is in order.

A problem faced by a minority party is recruiting candidates for higher offices. But this problem can be solved by steadily increasing the number of office holders from the party. These successful candidates for the same or higher offices stand as symbols of success. As such they can attract additional persons to the party as candidates and supporters. With three United States congressmen and thirty-three state legislators Republican sources have improved greatly recently. And just to get people to run is an important achievement for a minority party in a traditionally one-party state. North Carolina Republicans have had an increasing number of candidates.

The development of a plentiful supply of candidates also presents the possibility of factionalism in the party. As candidates and their followers eye the higher political stakes, they may differ on who has the better chance to win. These differences may lead to division within the party at the levels of both leaders and followers. A party in the minority cannot afford division. This not only divides the vote, but it also divides the party funds. Both are necessary to reach the voters and mobilize a majority.

Republican factionalism or potential factionalism has already been witnessed in the state. In 1962 the Republican party achieved great success in Guilford county, which contains Greensboro and High Point. It won all the seats in the state legislature and several local offices. However, these impressive victories were followed by a split in the county Republican organization. In 1964 and 1966 Republicans not only fell far short of the 1962 wins but also experienced difficulty in recruiting candidates to fill their slates.

Part of the Guilford factionalism was projected to the statewide gubernatorial primary which Republicans held in 1964. In that contest Reverend Charles Strong of Greensboro made a bid for the nomination against what he considered to be the hand-picked candidate of the Republican leadership, Robert Gavin. While bitterness did occur, the party got through the primary without an extremely tense internal battle. As Republicans surveyed the 1966 election and prepared for the 1968 gubernatorial campaign, speculation about a possible party split in selecting a candidate for the state's highest executive post has been widespread. The possibility of a primary contest with public disagreements between Republicans could attract attention to the minority party. However, it could also have mixed effects on its electoral hopes.

Strong competition for political offices at several levels and occasional victories have important consequences for minority party organization. As Republicans bid for local and statewide offices and as they compete with greater hope in the presidential races, they can improve the strength of the local parties. As was mentioned in Chapter Two, Republican county and precinct organization in the state is not complete. It varies greatly in sophistication. Increased competition should improve both the quantity and quality of such local efforts.

The presence of party members in public office and of party organization in many localities provides means for attracting attention to the party's program and personnel. A rostrum for stating positions on issues of state and local interest comes with public office. Furthermore, publicity by the minority party may force a stand by the opposition. For example, in the 1967 General Assembly Republicans received statewide coverage on a number of programs and issues. Individually and collectively, Republican legislators discussed topics such as electoral machinery, selection of county school boards, election of superior court judges, state civil service, constitutional reform, and others. Additionally, Republicans had enough strength in the House of Representatives to call for a roll-call vote on any bill and cast deciding votes on major issues. Though they were not successful in securing passage of their legislative program, they did and can have an influence on the program which is enacted.

North Carolina has experienced increased urbanization and industrialization with the locus of much of this activity in the central Piedmont section. The fact was also mentioned that reapportionment and redistricting have resulted in increased legislative representation for the Piedmont. Finally, recent research indicates that Republicans have received an increasing amount of support from urban areas over the last several decades. All of this adds up to the fact that competition is likely to grow significantly in these areas.

During recent elections North Carolinians have heard much about the need for a two-party system. Republicans have frequently instructed the state's citizens on the advantages of two parties and the disadvantages of one-party control. The argument usually conveys the idea that more responsible government and more significant achievements come when two major parties compete for office. The 1962 Republican platform makes the position clear:

This state has been unable to utilize its potential because of the one-party system of government exhibited by the Democratic party in the last sixty years. When any political party is too long in power, it becomes primarily interested in its own perpetuation without primary regard to the best interest of the people.

This quotation of course is concerned about the interest of North Carolinians and about future Democratic dominance. The latter subject deserves our attention now.

The Democratic party does have responsibility for much if not all of what North Carolina is. Democratic administrations and legislatures have controlled the state's governmental machinery. Their decisions have played a significant role in the social and economic character of the state. In other words, the Democratic party can pride itself on the state's accomplishments that have come under its direction. But it must also recognize and realize the shortcomings of the state and take blame for what progress has not been made. In education, industrial development, highway construction, tax policy, civil service, social welfare, urban renewal, and other areas the balance sheet must be examined for both credits and debits. This presents a dilemma for the state's majority party. In confronting the criticism that comes from a viable opposition, the Democratic party must not only extol its virtues and the state's accomplishments. It must also be willing to recognize areas of improvement and change which will be in the interest of the state. Such recognition may be bitter from time to time, but it may also preserve the party's strong position. Programs should not be devised on the basis of their effect on the internal squabblings of the party. Their objectives and standards should be in the state's interest.

Another new concern that Democrats have is whether they can afford the intraparty competition that has characterized races for major offices. Along with this concern must come the question of whether public battles between Democrats fought in the primaries will continue to be an acceptable way of determining nominees for political office. Does the development of a more capable minority party call for changes within the majority party?

Recently Democrats have been publicly stating that the 1968 gubernatorial race might be a good time for the Democrats to show unity. There has been talk that the party could select its nominee without serious opposition and possibly without a primary contest. Such discussion foresees benefits from Democratic accord in the face of a strong Republican challenge in 1968. Many Democrats recall the bitterness of primary competition in 1960 and 1964. Party unity will be more likely achieved through pre-primary maneuvering among factions than by abolishing the primary as the nominating device. The hope would be to present in the primary a candidate supported by a broadly based majority of Democrats rather than factional candidates receiving votes from narrow minorities. It may be necessary to attempt unity for offices in addition to governor, especially United States Senator and congressmen. A party that faces opposition frequently voices need for unity. Achieving unity through widely acceptable candidates is more difficult.

With increased competition does the party need to revise its organization and campaign activities? In recent years major spokesmen in the majority party have said that a new look at campaign techniques and appeals is necessary. More modern, sophisticated, and aggressive means of motivating voters must be sought. Enlightened and progressive programs must be advocated because now another party is in the contest and is appealing for support. More personal appeal involving many more people in campaigning might be helpful. Door-to-door, person-to-person campaigning might supplement or replace the nonpersonal political rally. A greater and more ingenious use of television might combine the need for both a personal approach and wide coverage. Court house politics depending on a few "important contacts" might be de-emphasized as the political maturity of the voter is recognized. An active program to recruit new voters and workers for the party would certainly be beneficial.

Two features of state politics must be the common concern of Democrats and Republicans. Both parties must recognize the changing age of the electorate. About half of the voters in the state are below thirty-five. Many of these voters have great demands and high expectations. Issues, candidates, and programs must be chosen with these basic facts in mind. Most congressional candidates of one party in a recent election were below forty. As many young citizens qualify to be voters, they must choose between alternative parties, and the choices made as they enter the political world will have enduring effect on party alignment. Some new voters will contribute to the parties more substantially by volunteering time in party campaigns, contributing ideas on issues and programs, and, indeed, offering themselves as candidates for offices at all levels. Traditional political allegiances will share the political stage with new voters and their recently determined preferences.

A second common problem is political apathy. Political parties as major vehicles of popular government should find new ways and intensify old ways of encouraging people to participate in politics. Means must be devised to encourage active participation in campaigning on behalf of individual candidates and party slates. Volunteer workers must be recruited not only to expand popular involvement but also to reduce political costs. More part-time but whole-hearted partisans are needed to man the headquarters and staffs which are necessary to political contests. And while greater participation should be expected around election time, a continuing interest and sustaining commitment between elections is basic to the health of political parties and democracy. Increased involvement should also include broadening the financial base on which parties and candidates depend. New ideas are necessary to solicit funds from an increasing and increasingly diverse number of persons. It is likely that if individuals invest even minimally in partisan combat, they will recognize their stake in it. Whether the investment is by money, energy, time, or emotional commitment, the stakes are high for political parties and for democracy.

LIST OF ADDITIONAL READINGS

For readers who would like additional materials on North Carolina politics, either as a special subject or within the context of Southern politics, the following books are suggested:

Cole, Taylor, and Hallowell, John H. (eds.). *The Southern Political Scene, 1938-1948.* Gainesville, Florida: The Journal of Politics, 1948.

Cosman, Bernard. *Five States For Goldwater: Continuity and Change in Southern Presidential Voting Patterns.* University, Alabama: University of Alabama Press, 1966.

Crotty, William J. "The Role of the County Chairman in the Contemporary Party System in North Carolina." Unpublished Ph. D. dissertation, The University of North Carolina at Chapel Hill, 1964.

Election Laws of the State of North Carolina, 1966. Raleigh: The State Board of Elections, 1966.

Gatlin, Douglas S. "Socio-Economic Bases of Party Competition: A Case Study of North Carolina." Unpublished Ph. D. dissertation, The University of North Carolina at Chapel Hill, 1964.

Heard, Alexander. *A Two-Party South?* Chapel Hill: The University of North Carolina Press, 1952.

Hodges, Luther. *Businessman in the Statehouse: Six Years as Governor of North Carolina.* Chapel Hill: The University of North Carolina Press, 1962.

Jewell, Malcolm E. *Legislative Representation in the Contemporary South.* Durham, North Carolina: Duke University Press, 1967.

Key, V. O. Jr. *Southern Politics in State and Nation.* New York: Alfred A. Knopf, Inc., 1949.

Lefler, Hugh Talmage, and Newsome, Albert Ray. *North Carolina: The History of a Southern State.* Rev. Ed. Chapel Hill: The University of North Carolina Press, 1963.

Leiserson, Avery (ed.). *The American South in the 1960's.* New York: Frederick A. Praeger, 1964.

Lewis, Henry W. *Primary and General Election Law and Procedure—1966.* Chapel Hill: The Institute of Government, The University of North Carolina at Chapel Hill, 1966.

Matthews, Donald R., and others (compilers). *North Carolina Votes: General Election Returns, by County for President of the United States, 1868-1960; Governor of North Carolina, 1868-1960; and United States Senator from North Carolina, 1914-1960.* Chapel Hill: The University of North Carolina Press, 1962.

Matthews, Donald R. and Prothro, James W. *Negroes and the New Southern Politics.* New York: Harcourt, Brace & World, Inc., 1966.

Puryear, Elmer L. *Democratic Party Dissension in North Carolina, 1928-1936.* Chapel Hill: The University of North Carolina Press, 1962.

Rankin, Robert S. *The Government and Administration of North Carolina.* New York: Thomas Y. Crowell Company, 1955.

Sanford, Terry. *But What About the People?* New York: Harper & Row, Publishers, Inc., 1966.

Sindler, Allan P. *Change in the Contemporary South.* Durham, North Carolina: Duke University Press, 1963.

Strong, Donald S. *Urban Republicanism in the South.* University, Alabama: Bureau of Public Administration, University of Alabama, 1960.